History and Traditions of the
UNT Health Science Center
at Fort Worth

Published by the University of North Texas Health Science Center, Fort Worth, Texas

Printed in the United States of America

Editorial Committee

> Scott B. Ransom, DO, MBA, MPH, President — Executive Editor
> Mark Baker, DO, Class of 1976, North Texas Radiology, Fort Worth, Texas
> Sam Buchanan, DO, Class of 1975, Special Advisor to the President
> Claudia Coggin, PhD, Assistant Professor, Social and Behavioral Science, School of Public Health
> Robert DeLuca, DO, Class of 1984, Private practice, Eastland, Texas
> Craig Elam, MLS, Senior Director Collection Development, Gibson D. Lewis Health Science Library
> James Froelich, III, DO, Class of 1981, Family Care Clinic, Bonham, Texas
> Russell Gamber, DO, MPH, Professor of Manipulative Medicine
> Danny Jensen, Vice President for Governmental Affairs
> Robert Kaman, JD, PhD, Associate Dean for Graduate Studies, Graduate School of Biomedical Sciences
> Monte Troutman, DO, Associate Professor, Internal Medicine
> Stanley Weiss, DO, Associate Professor, Family Medicine
> Thomas Yorio, PhD, Provost and Executive Vice President for Academic Affairs and Research
> Eugene Zachary, DO, Associate Professor, Family Medicine

Editorial Director: Charles Tips

Senior Editor: Jean Tips

Design Director: Carl Bluemel

Photographers: Tommy Hawkes, Matt Havlik, Amy Buresh, Jeremy Enlow, Deborah Brashear, Dana Russell

ISBN 978-0-9825351-8-9

UNT Health Science Center
at Fort Worth

Vision:
To become a Top 10 health science center

Mission:
To improve the health and quality of life for the people of Texas and beyond through
excellence in education, research, clinical care and community engagement
and to provide national leadership in primary care.

Table of Contents

Timeline

TCOM opens as a private college of osteopathic medicine with an entering class of 20 students.

First rural clinic opens in Justin, Texas.

Three osteopathic physicians, D. D. Beyer, George Luibel and Carl Everett, procure a charter from the State of Texas for the Texas College of Osteopathic Medicine.
1966

TCOM hires Henry B. Hardt, PhD, as its first dean.

First faculty are hired: Elizabeth (Libby) Harris, PhD, in microbiology and Mary Lu Schunder, MA, in anatomy.
1970

North Texas State University agrees to provide basic science instruction to first- and second-year medical students in Denton.
1972

First 18 graduates receive their Doctor of Osteopathy (DO) degrees.
1974

Ground is broken for the first permanent building on campus, designated Medical Education Building 1.
1976

1960　　　1965　　　1970　1971　1972　1973　1974　1975　1976　1977

1961
Committee meets to investigate the feasibility of establishing an osteopathic medical school in Texas.

1969
C. Ray Stokes, director of development, is hired as the first employee.

1971
First state funds are received when Senate Bill 160 is approved, allowing TCOM to contract with the State of Texas to educate osteopathic medical students.

A renovated bowling alley on Camp Bowie Boulevard houses classrooms, basic science laboratories and administrative offices.

1973
Marion E. Coy, DO, becomes the first president of the institution.

First community outpatient clinic opens on Rosedale Avenue in Fort Worth.

1975
TCOM becomes a state-supported medical school, separate from North Texas State University but under the jurisdiction of the NTSU Board of Regents.

Ralph Willard, DO, is hired as vice president for Academic Affairs and dean of TCOM.

TCOM receives full accreditation from the American Osteopathic Association.

1977
The basic sciences program moves from Denton to leased space in the River Plaza office park in Fort Worth.

The Founders' Medal is established to recognize "significant contributions to healthcare and/or osteopathic medical education."

The eight-story Medical Education Building 1 opens, consolidating the basic science and clinical didactic teaching programs in Fort Worth, as well as housing the library and administrative offices.
1978

"Design of the Medical Curriculum in Relation to the Health Needs of the Nation" is issued by TCOM's Task Force on Educational Goals. This groundbreaking goals statement calls for increased attention to nutrition, lifestyle and other aspects of preventive medicine in the medical curriculum, in addition to traditional medical teaching.
1980

Medical Education Building 2 opens, providing classrooms, basic science offices, laboratories and animal facilities.
1982

Ground is broken for the third major building on campus, Medical Education Building 3.

"Research in the osteopathic medical school: a statement of the research goals of TCOM" is issued, calling for increased emphasis on basic and clinical research as a vital component of the institution.
1984

David Richards, DO, becomes the institution's third president.

Medical Education Building 3 opens, housing a state-of-the-art library, computing services and biomedical communications.
1986

The Robert L. Thompson Strategic Hospital at Carswell Air Force Base becomes the 12th affiliated teaching hospital, a model of civilian-military cooperation.
1988

1978   1979   1980   1981   1982   1983   1984   1985   1986   1987   1988

1979
The Cowtown Marathon is established, co-sponsored by the Institute for Human Fitness.

1981
Ralph Willard, DO, becomes the institution's second president.

Ground is broken for a biomedical research facility, Medical Education Building 2.

The institution becomes a member of the Association of Academic Health Centers.

1985
The school co-sponsors and hosts the first 12-county high school art competition, the largest high school art competition in North Texas.

1987
"Responsibilities to the institution, the community, and the profession: a statement of the service goals of TCOM" is issued, recognizing the importance of community service, as well as service to professional organizations and continuing medical education.

The institution becomes the first medical school in Texas to have a smoke-free environment.

The DNA Identity Laboratory is created with a special state appropriation to reduce a backlog of paternity cases pending in state courts.

The UNT Press publishes *Texas College of Osteopathic Medicine: The First Twenty Years*, by C. Ray Stokes and Judy Alter, documenting the institution's history.
1990

The North Texas Eye Research Institute becomes the first research institute on campus.
1992

A contract is established with the US Bureau of Prisons to provide health services for inmates at the new Federal Medical Center, Carswell.

The Graduate School of Biomedical Sciences awards its first doctoral degrees in biomedical sciences.
1994

With a grant from the Arnold P. Gold Foundation, UNTHSC holds its first White Coat Ceremony. The ceremony is a "rite of passage" for students that encourages a psychological contract for professionalism and empathy.

The Health Science Center and UNT College of Music collaborate to form the Texas Center for Music and Medicine.
1996

UNTHSC and the University of Texas at Dallas sign an affiliation agreement to establish a BS/DO dual-degree program whereby eligible students can obtain their undergraduate and a Doctor of Osteopathic Medicine degree in seven years.
1998

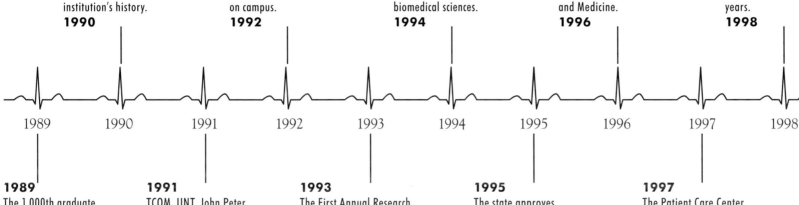

1989   1990   1991   1992   1993   1994   1995   1996   1997   1998   1999

1989
The 1,000th graduate receives a diploma.

1991
TCOM, UNT, John Peter Smith Hospital, Harris Methodist Hospitals and UT Southwestern Medical School combine to form the Tarrant County Medical Education Consortium.

1993
The First Annual Research Appreciation Day provides an opportunity for students, faculty and staff to share their research efforts.

The Texas Higher Education Coordinating Board approves establishment of the Graduate School of Biomedical Sciences.

TCOM is officially redesignated and expanded by the State of Texas as the University of North Texas Health Science Center.

1995
The state approves a new Bachelor's degree in the Physician Assistant Studies program.

1997
The Patient Care Center opens, housing all campus clinics.

The Physician Assistant Studies program (PA) admits its first students.

1999
The Physician Assistant Studies program graduates its first class.

The School of Public Health is founded.

UNTHSC joins the UNT Denton and Dallas campuses to form the University of North Texas System.

UNTHSC co-sponsors the first Hispanic Wellness Fair in Fort Worth. The fair attracts 75 providers and 1,000 participants.

The UNTHSC School of Public Health collaborates with the City of Fort Worth Public Health Department to establish the first African-American Health Fair.

The Physician Assistant Studies program receives approval to offer the Master of Physician Assistant Studies (MPAS) degree.

OSTMED®, the world's first comprehensive index to the literature of osteopathic medicine, is inaugurated.

For the first time, TCOM is ranked among the Top 50 medical schools in the nation in primary care by *US News & World Report.*

The Center for BioHealth opens, dedicated primarily to biotechnology and public health. It is the first HSC academic building to be built with a combination of public and private funds.

Alumni Plaza is dedicated.

UNTHSC and JPS establish the first Federally Qualitified Health Center (FQHC) in Fort Worth

The Osteopathic Medical Center of Fort Worth (OMCT) closes due to bankruptcy.

UNT Health is established as the faculty clinical practice for UNTHSC.

Scott Ransom, DO, MBA, MPH, becomes the institution's fifth president.

The Texas Center for Health Disparities at UNTHSC hosts its first Health Disparities Conference, with more than 150 attendees.

As part of the Master Plan, demolition of the Osteopathic Medical Center of Texas (OMCT) facility is completed and ground cleared for construction of the new Medical Education and Training Building.

The TECH Fort Worth Acceleration Lab is established.

UNTHSC establishes and convenes a Board of Visitors as a strategic advisory group.

The Institute for Cancer and Blood Disorders is established.

The 112,000-square-foot Medical Education and Training Building opens.

UNTHSC receives Best in Texas rankings in Family Medicine, Geriatric Medicine, Rural Medicine and Primary Care by *U.S. News & World Report.*

The Inaugural class of Rural Osteopathic Medical Education (ROME) graduates.

The Doctor of Physical Therapy (DPT) program enters its first students.

The Doctor of Philosophy (PhD) degree is established in the School of Public Health

Lt. Gen. Ronald R. Blanck, DO, becomes the institution's fourth president.

2000

2002

2004

2006

2008

2010

2000 2001 2002 2003 2004 2005 2006 2007 2008 2009 2010

2001
The Osteopathic Research Center (ORC) is founded to foster nationwide collaborative research on the efficacy of osteopathic manipulative medicine.

The Texas Missing Persons DNA Database is established at UNTHSC with funding from the Texas State Attorney General's Crime Victims Compensation Fund.

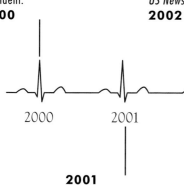

2003
UNTHSC enrollment exceeds 1,000 students.

A self-insurance malpractice plan is established for the clinical practice.

For the first time, the Physician Assistant Studies program is nationally ranked 33rd and the Geriatrics program is ranked 15th in their respective programs by *US News & World Report.*

2005
UNTHSC reaches an agreement with the Tarrant County Hospital District to provide clinical services to John Peter Smith Hospital and the JPS Health Network.

UNTHSC purchases the former OMCT property, doubling the size of the campus.

UNTHSC establishes the Texas Center for Health Disparities (TCHD), one of the NIH-designated EXPORT Centers.

2007
The School of Health Professions enrolls its first students.

The First Annual Employee Appreciation Day is established.

The Institute for Aging and Alzheimer's Disease Research (IAADR) is founded.

The Osteopathic Heritage Foundation Musculoskeletal Research Laboratory is established.

The Center for Community Health is established.

FOR HER, a collaborative health model for women of all ages, is founded.

2009
The Doctor of Physical Therapy (DPT) program is established.

The Center for Learning and Development is established to teach faculty how to be better teachers.

The Department of Pediatrics partnership with Cook Children's Health Care System is established.

The Master of Health Administration (MHA) is established.

UNT Health implements an Electronic Medical Record System (EMR).

The Evolution of Institutional Leadership

Founders

Name	Title	Dates
George J. Luibel, DO	Founder, Chairman of the Board of Directors	1966-1975
D. D. "Danny" Beyer, DO	Founder, Vice Chairman of the Board of Directors	1966-1975
Carl E. Everett, DO	Founder, Secretary-Treasurer of the Board of Directors	1966-1975

Texas College of Osteopathic Medicine – Deans and Presidents

Henry B. Hardt, PhD	Founding Dean	1970-1973
Marion E. Coy, DO	President	1973-1975
Ralph L. Willard, DO	Dean	1975-1985
	President	1981-1985
T. Eugene Zachary, DO	Dean	1984-1990
David M. Richards, DO	President	1986-1993
Benjamin L. Cohen, DO	Dean	1991-1993

University of North Texas Health Science Center – Presidents

David M. Richards, DO	President	1993-1999
Lt. Gen. Ronald R. Blanck, DO	President	2000-2006
Scott B. Ransom, DO, MBA, MPH	President	2006-

University of North Texas Health Science Center – Provosts

Benjamin L. Cohen, DO	Provost	2000-2002
Thomas Yorio, PhD	Provost	2008-

Texas College of Osteopathic Medicine – Deans

Benjamin L. Cohen, DO	Dean	1993-1999
Deborah Blackwell, DO	Acting Dean	2000-2001
Marc B. Hahn, DO	Dean	2001-2008
Alan Podawiltz, DO, MS	Acting Dean	2008-2009
Donald N. Peska, DO, MEd	Dean	2009-

Graduate School of Biomedical Sciences – Deans

Thomas Yorio, PhD	Founding Dean	1993-2007
Jamboor Vishwanatha, PhD	Dean	2007-

School of Public Health – Deans

Fernando Treviño, PhD, MPH	Founding Dean	1996-2007
Richard S. Kurz, PhD	Dean	2007-

School of Health Professions – Deans

J. Warren Anderson, EdD	Founding Dean	2007-

UNT Health – Presidents

Randall Jones, MPA	President	2007-2008
Kathleen Forbes, MD, MMM	President	2008-

North Texas State University – Presidents and Chancellors

C. C. "Jitter" Nolen	President	1975-1979
John L. Carter, Jr	Acting President	1979-1980
Frank E. Vandiver, PhD	President	1980-1981
	Chancellor	1981
Howard W. Smith, Jr	Acting Chancellor	1981-1982
Alfred F. Hurley, PhD	Chancellor	1982-1988

University of North Texas – Chancellors

Alfred F. Hurley, PhD	Chancellor	1988-2002
Lee Jackson, MPA	Chancellor	2002-

A Glimpse of Our 40-Year History

By Scott B. Ransom,
DO, MBA, MPH

In 1970, we celebrated the first Earth Day, cheered the runners at New York City's first marathon and watched the first Boeing 747 take off. That jumbo jet wasn't the only impressive take-off that year. Three pioneering men began an institution that eventually would become the UNT Health Science Center, housed on a thriving 33-acre campus in Fort Worth's Cultural District.

The Texas College of Osteopathic Medicine (TCOM) was the founding school of the UNT Health Science Center and became the nation's seventh accredited osteopathic medical school. Our journey began in rented quarters on an empty hospital floor and soon moved into a barely renovated bowling alley to support the first class of 20 motivated students. While the small faculty was supported by very limited and precarious financial resources, the institution received a boost when it became a state-supported institution in 1975. With state support came much-needed resources to support a more robust faculty and the construction of the first major medical education building in 1978.

The institution offered only one degree until 1993, when it became a full-fledged health science center. Health science center status also brought more state support and inspired a broader vision by adding more degree programs to help support the creation of a thriving campus of nearly 1,600 students and 400 faculty that now boasts not only a nationally recognized medical school, but also the Graduate School of Biomedical Sciences, the School of Public Health and the School of Health Professions — all of them earning their own impressive credentials.

The Graduate School of Biomedical Sciences (GSBS) was founded in 1993 and became the second school of the UNT Health Science Center with the addition of the MS and PhD Biomedical Science degree programs. The launching of the Graduate School sparked intellectual curiosity and the vigor that would improve the quality of the institution's biomedical education and expand the investigative capabilities to become Texas' fastest-growing research institution. By 2009, investigation blossomed to include 12 dedicated research centers and institutes that would set the stage for national prominence in all campus programs.

The School of Public Health was founded in 1999. The school would become the nation's 33rd accredited school of public health and help expand the institution's commitment to improving the health of the entire community. The growing school would complement the entire institution with the addition of several degree offerings – the MPH in 1996 (started in GSBS), the DrPH in 1999, the MHA in 2009 and the PhD in 2010.

The School of Health Professions enrolled its first students in 2007 with the addition of the Department of Physician Assistant Studies. While the MPAS degree program was founded as part of

Student Enrollment – 1970-2010

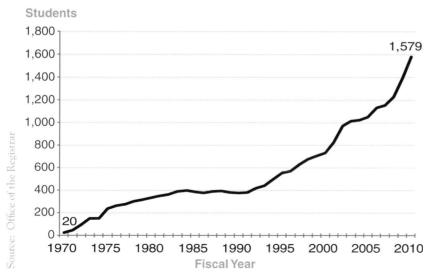

Degree Offerings by School

Texas College of Osteopathic Medicine	DO 1970			
Graduate School of Biomedical Science	MS 1993	PhD 1993		
School of Public Health	MPH 1996	DrPH 1999	MHA 2009	PhD 2010
School of Health Professions	MPAS 2000	DPT 2010		
MD School	MD Under Development			

Construction begins on Med Ed 1 as seen in 1977. The bowling alley is in the foreground, and Fort Worth Osteopathic Hospital is visible to the upper right.

reorganized and professionally managed, then it quadrupled in size and quickly became the largest multidisciplinary clinical practice in Tarrant County, UNT Health.

In 2010, we celebrated the 40th anniversary in a time of continued growth and achievement in all areas of our mission. We have much for which to be proud and thankful. Our campus has grown from a bowling alley to a modern, 1.2 million-square foot facility with state-of-the-art laboratories, classrooms and clinical facilities. Approximately 400 full-time and 800 adjunct faculty support nine degree programs and a rapidly growing research and clinical footprint to help solve critical health care challenges for the State of Texas. In 2010, we were nationally recognized for excellence in many areas, including 19th for primary care medical schools, 11th for Family Medicine, 15th for Geriatrics Medicine, 22nd for Rural Medicine and 33rd for Physician Assistant Studies by *U.S. News & World Report*. We are now engaged with Fort Worth and Tarrant County to simultaneously help support our community's health and institutional programs. The past 40 years have created the platform for an inspiring story of success, disappointment, courage, adversity and national prominence.

TCOM in 1997, the program moved to a school dedicated to the education and development of allied health professionals in 2008. The Department of Physical Therapy was also added in 2009 and welcomed its first DPT students the following year.

The bankruptcy of the Osteopathic Medical Center (OMCT) of Fort Worth and the closure of all osteopathic hospitals in Texas simultaneously created organizational vulnerability and opportunity. While the first TCOM classes and most clinical education were supported by OMCT until 2004, the closure of these facilities set the foundation for the UNT Health Science Center to partner and collaborate with most local hospitals and start its own dedicated clinical practice. In 2007, a relatively small physician practice was

Navigating our Story

On the following pages, you'll read the straightforward chronological facts of "life"— the ups and downs encountered by any organization fortunate enough to have 40 years behind them. It's the personal recollections and stories of those years that give spark to those facts, as well as explanation. You'll see those plus photos of leaders, faculty, staff and students throughout.

Some themes you will see continue over time: vision, perseverance and dedication to students and to Texans. Just like the maverick city we sit in, you will see we have always done things a bit differently ... and probably always will.

Research Awards – 1971-2010

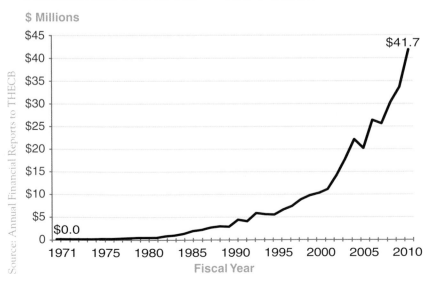

Fulltime Faculty and Staff – 1969-2010

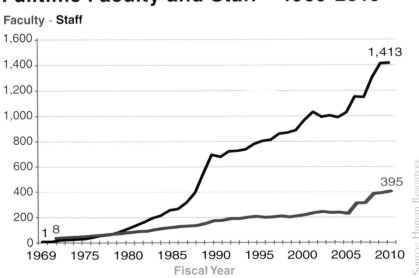

First, our section "Beginning" examines the tremendous vision, courage and commitment of some scrappy individuals and supporters who poured their hearts, minds and money into founding something special … not to mention the students and faculty who stepped into the unknown with those visionaries.

"A Leap of Faith" covers the journey from conception to the first day of class as a private school, including our early association with the Osteopathic Medical Center of Texas. "Humble Beginnings," by former TCOM Communications Director Judy Alter, portrays the austere surroundings of the "O" fifth floor and the bowling alley; and "Teaching Tales" highlights some of the classroom high jinks that lent levity to a tight-belt enterprise.

Deeply rooted in our past, of course, is our osteopathic heritage and its philosophy of treating the whole person. In that spirit, to give you a sense of where our school fits in the broader profession historically, we include the "Seven Turning Points of Osteopathic Medicine," a brief history of osteopathic medicine and its founder, A. T. Still, by TCOM Professor Russell Gamber, DO, MPH. Finally, we have always maintained a collaborative approach and commitment to community involvement — the "Fort Worth Way." No history of our school could be without mention of the history of the great city with which we find ourselves more and more engaged. That section is appropriately titled "Mavericks in a Maverick Town," by TCOM class of 1984 alumnus Robert DeLuca, DO.

"Yesterday" is a section that describes our arrival as a public, state-assisted school through our "marriage" to North Texas State University, as well as our evolution to a true health science center with the addition of the Graduate School of Biomedical Sciences and then other schools. In "A Health Science Center Emerges," the campus and student body growth and diversification are chronicled, and "Bursting at the Seams" gives a glimpse into student life at that time. Growth of the institution also brought the slow acceptance of our physician faculty among other health care professionals. It

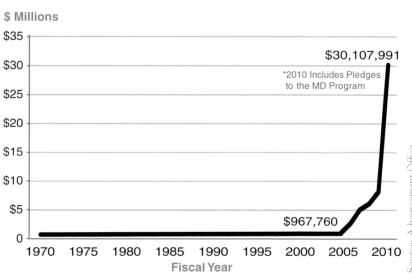

▲
Class of 1975 class officers: president Clint Burns, vice president Roger Hamilton, treasurer Robert Wilson and secretary Peggy Hall (Stenger).

wasn't an easy path to parity, and "Stumbling Blocks to Stepping Stones," by TCOM class of 1975 alumnus and former chair of Surgery Sam Buchanan, DO, shows how we overcame "town-gown" and partnership conflicts to build alliances, not just in health care delivery, but in research and academics as well. During these years, we innovated in community wellness and prevention, as related in " An Eye on Prevention," by long-time faculty members Stanley Weiss, DO, and Robert Kaman, JD, PhD, who started the Cowtown Marathon, a Fort Worth tradition.

The "Today" section follows our progress since we entered the millennium as a dynamic center poised to make great gains in key areas. "The Health Science Center Today," by Vice President

Patient Encounters – 1971-2010

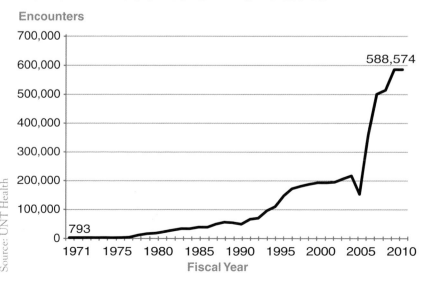

Encounters

588,574

793

Source: UNT Health

Fiscal Year

Gifts – 1971-2010

$ Millions

$30,107,991

*2010 Includes Pledges to the MD Program

$967,760

Source: Advancement Office

Fiscal Year

of Marketing and Communications Jean Tips, shows that much is now in sharp contrast to the early years. State-of-the-art facilities, technology and curriculum have come a long way. We have organized our research into specific areas of focus. School enrollment, extramural research awards and patient care delivery all have skyrocketed.

While those things have changed, students have kept very specific traditions, from the formal White Coat and Commencement activities to more informal events and celebrations such as the DO Dash and Casino Night. They continue to maintain active service to the community, as shown throughout the photos of "Prescription for Tomorrow." With overall growth of the organization, support teams of various types are even more essential and provide a solid foundation of which the early staff would be envious. "Teams of Excellence" shows just some of the people who make everything run smoothly in support of our core missions. We work to remain actively engaged in our community and in close touch with Austin, as seen in "Blessed with Support" and "Working with Austin." Most important to our increasingly diverse state, we make sure we offer opportunities in science to the widest diversity of students at all levels. "Diversity Built In" describes our programs for students of all ages and some teachers, too. "Centers of Excellence" describes our inter-professional Health Institutes of Texas.

The "Tomorrow" section explains how we are positioning ourselves to see further payoff in our next 40 years. "Ensuring a Bright Future" presents our plan to support the health care needs of Texas, where growth has outstripped the state's ability to provide enough health providers of all kinds, especially in rural and underserved areas. It is also a timely plan nationally, at a point when increasing competition for research funding demands focus and excellence. This kind of strategic planning includes our campus facilities, and "Room to Grow," by Senior Vice President of Community Engagement Greg Upp, lays out our Master Plan for campus growth. Finally, we describe our goals for the future, which focus on excellence, continuous improvement and empowerment, in "Adapting While Leading," by Executive Vice President and Provost Thomas Yorio, PhD.

Prepare for a fascinating journey as you browse our history and our current work and peer into the future through the pages of this book. We look forward to an exciting next forty years!

▲
Osteopathic family physician Clifton Cage has worked extensively with the US Department of Veterans Affairs' Community-Based Outpatient Clinic and as a principal investigator for numerous clinical trials.

UNT | HEALTH SCIENCE CENTER™

At its August 2010 quarterly meeting, the UNT System Board of Regents approved a new graphic identity to provide a more unified look for all system components — the System office, UNT Denton, UNT Health Science Center at Fort Worth and UNT Dallas. All four logos were redesigned to share the UNT acronym, the same type font and the same shade of green.

In taking this action, the UNT System became the first university system in the state to use a consistent color and look for all its member logos.

The new logo is being implemented in Fall 2010. While our future is highlighted in green, historical sections inside show our original red look.

Prior to this change, UNTHSC had been represented over the years by various versions of the Texas College of Osteopathic Medicine branding depicting the Staff of Aesculapius, with its single entwined serpent, the ancient symbol for medical healing. Starting in late 1993 with the health science center established, a stylized version of the snake was designed by Katrinka Blickle Pellecchia in Biomedical Communications. That version—a mark fondly referred to as the "snake on a stick"—has served as the institution's logo until now.

1976
Roxanne
Cothern

1993
Katrinka
Blickle
Pellecchia

▲

A rare sight in Fort Worth! Snow blankets the campus on February 11, 2010, leading to an even rarer cancellation of classes.

Top right: Workers mount the EAD eighth-floor History Wall, predecessor to this book.

Right: Our 40th Anniversary banners line Camp Bowie Boulevard.

Lower right: June Coleman, telephone voice of the HSC, views art in the Atrium Gallery.

Below: Looking down the great divide of the new MET auditorium.

View of campus in the early 1970s: Classes in 1970-71 were held on the fifth floor of the Fort Worth Osteopathic Hospital on Montgomery Street. The administrative offices were in the small white house on the corner with Mattison Avenue (to the right). The second-story garage apartment housing the anatomy lab is on the far right. The hospital ceased operations in 2004 and eventually was demolished to make way for the Medical Education and Training Building (see opposite). The Education and Administration Building has stood in the space occupied by the houses and buildings in this photograph's foreground since 1978.

The Health Science Center campus today: Looking west along red-brick Camp Bowie Boulevard, all six major buildings on campus are clearly visible. In the foreground stands the Center for BioHealth, beyond which is the red-roofed Research and Education Building (formerly Med Ed 2) and the Education and Administration Building (EAD, formerly Med Ed 1). The Medical Education and Training Building, which opened in 2010, occupies top-center position. The Gibson D. Lewis Library Building (formerly Med Ed 3) is to the right, with the Patient Care Center to its right. The campus master plan calls for another 11 buildings to be erected on the 33-acre campus.

In its second year of operation, the Texas College of Osteopathic Medicine was housed in the former Tavener's Playdium Bowling Alley, just one of many resourceful adaptations as the school embarked, limited in every respect but optimism.

BEGINNING

The nation turned after World War II to the building of new hospitals and then, in the mid-1960s, began the first great wave of medical school foundings in more than 50 years. Osteopathic physicians in Texas pushed for their school to take root in Fort Worth, a city that offered the combination of civic-mindedness, visionary effort, can-do spirit, private enterprise and public support to help it flourish.

Who at the time could have guessed that such austere beginnings would realize the benefits to the City of Fort Worth and the people of Texas?

Museum of Osteopathic Medicine℠, Kirksville, MO [PH 446]

▲
Osteopathic medicine was developed in 1874 by Andrew Taylor Still, who stated: "Any variation from health has a cause, and the cause has a location. It is the business of the osteopathic physician to locate and remove it, doing away with the disease and getting healthy instead."

A LEAP OF FAITH

The challenge of starting a DO school from scratch

Wayne Stockseth

Sam Ganz, DO

Wayne O. Stockseth is what is known in Texas as a rainmaker, someone with the political and financial clout to make good things happen for worthy enterprises. Thanks to a longtime relationship with his physician, Sam Ganz, DO, in Corpus Christi, Stockseth was also a believer in the value of osteopathic medicine.

In his words, "When Sam approached me to be the only non-DO on the start-up board of an osteopathic college, I was delighted but skeptical. There had to be lots of better ways to get a medical school going than by starting from scratch. We drove up to Fort Worth to meet with the founding team, and within 10 minutes I was convinced that it not only could be done but that it should be done and *would* be done. George [Luibel] was the strength. He'd been at the AOA and carried a lot of weight. He had the executive ability to get people to pull their oars together. Carl [Everett] and Danny [Beyer] were very capable lieutenants to George."

George Luibel and (Daniel) D.D. Beyer had been on the founding team at Fort Worth Osteopathic Hospital on Summit Avenue, started in 1946. Carl Everett came along to lend his talents in 1949. All three would remain instrumental in the hospital, including the building of a permanent location on Montgomery Street, opened in 1956. Fort Worth "O," as the hospital was affectionately known, had galvanized the Fort Worth osteopathic community, it had given it prominence throughout the state of Texas and within the osteopathic profession nationwide.

All of this collaborative success had led to camaraderie within the team. On social occasions, talk would turn to the subject of the next goal, an osteopathic medical school. For one thing, from before World War I until long after World War II, there had been a lull in the opening of new medical schools, including osteopathic colleges. It was time to get things going again. The American Osteopathic Association (AOA) had given out a siren call that the profession would cease to grow without more schools. The AOA was shocked to learn the profession was shrinking — retirements exceeded graduations. Additionally, curious events in California in 1962 had

The TCOM Board of Directors grew in 1966 when John Burnett, DO, of Dallas (second from left) and Sam Ganz, DO, of Corpus Christi (opposite) joined founders (l-r) D.D. Beyer, George Luibel and Carl Everett. By 1968, the Board would expand to 12 members.

led to an osteopathic medical school being "given away" to become an MD-granting school, and all of that state's DOs were invited to become MDs. Some defensive shoring up was called for to prevent the same thing happening in Texas.

But the main factor driving talk of an osteopathic medical school in Fort Worth was the lack of one anywhere in the multi-state region. In order to increase the practice of osteopathic medicine in Texas, physicians resident in other states would have to be enticed to move to Texas. Alternatively, young students would have to be motivated to go to school far out of state for four and more years and then return (by 1969, the legislative appropriation, in a program worked out early in the decade by Elmer Baum, DO, of Austin, reached $100,000 in out-of-state scholarship support to 85 osteopathic students, despite the certainty that a number of them would not return to practice in Texas). This was exactly how Texas osteopathic practice had been growing since the 1890s, but it was no formula for a bright future.

In 1961, the Texas Association of Osteopathic Physicians and Surgeons (soon after Texas Osteopathic Medical Association) formed a committee to pursue the idea of founding the Texas College of Osteopathic Medicine. According to Luibel, who was on the committee, pursuit consisted of a brief meeting in someone's hotel room just prior to the TOMA board of trustees' semi-annual meeting, followed by a report to the trustees that the committee was still interested in establishing a school. When Luibel rotated into the chairmanship of the committee after four years, he was determined to take the bull by the horns. The committee recommended TOMA take action on a number of fronts, including forming a foundation to accept donations, beginning fundraising campaigns and undertaking studies of possible sites and potential alliances.

Abe M. Herman, JD, served as legal counsel for TCOM.

When TOMA failed to act on the recommendations, Luibel moved to disband the committee. At the same time, it was learned that the College of Osteopathic Medicine and Surgery in Des Moines, one of the five existing osteopathic schools, wanted to relocate. Officials of TOMA contacted the Iowa college, and a series of exploratory visits to Fort Worth ensued. Through his position on the AOA board of trustees, Luibel learned that Michigan College of Osteopathic Medicine was being built in Pontiac (soon after incorporated under Michigan State University in East Lansing). All of these developments caused Luibel and the other TOMA members to "do their homework," make contacts in the community, raise expectations and generally come to see the idea of an osteopathic school in Fort Worth as a realistic goal.

As Luibel expected, the city fathers of Des Moines, learning that their beloved 61-year-old institution was actively shopping around for a new home, made a compelling offer for the school to stay, where it does to this day as Des Moines University – College of Osteopathic Medicine. But a "homework" project had landed in Luibel's lap late in the process when a dean of the Iowa school asked him how they would go about acquiring a Texas charter. Fort Worth attorney Abe Herman informed Luibel that Texas, happily, did not require the substantial assets many states did and that a charter could be had for the cost of sending a lawyer to Austin plus the filing fee.

"Don't Call It Tee-Com!"

With "Texas College of Osteopathic Medicine" being something of a mouthful to use for each of the increasing number of phone calls, George Luibel decreed that it was permissible to answer the phone with a cheery "T-C-O-M." But don't dare say "Tee-Com." Made the college sound like a telephone company.

"Tee-Com" is the more prevalent usage these days; however, be aware there are plenty around who still wince on hearing it.

George J. Luibel

"Dr Luibel exemplifies the osteopathic philosophy in his every action. He has made an outstanding impact on the prestige of the osteopathic profession, and his teaching and leadership abilities are an inspiration to all who know him." So editorialized *Texas DO* magazine after George Luibel was named "Educator of the Year" at the American Osteopathic Association House of Delegates meeting in Florida in 1988.

Luibel was the first and only chairman, from 1966 to 1974, of the board of directors for the Texas College of Osteopathic Medicine. He was a president, vice president and trustee of the AOA and president of the Texas Osteopathic Medical Association as well as member of the board of trustees and of the House of Delegates and president of TOMA District 2. He was chief of staff at the Fort Worth Osteopathic Medical Center and president of the board. He served as president of the Kirksville College of Osteopathic Medicine Alumni Association. He held the chairmanship of the Board of Members of the Tarrant County Hospital District, the first DO to do so. He received TOMA's Distinguished Service Award, its highest honor. All that and he was president of the Sierra Club of Fort Worth.

Luibel was born in Springfield, Ohio. He earned his Doctor of Osteopathic Medicine degree from the Kirksville College of Osteopathic Medicine in 1936. He interned at Sparks Clinic and Hospital in Dallas. From there, he settled in Ennis, Texas, where in 1944 he married Mary Edwina Larmoyeaux, a registered nurse and lifelong helpmate, who served as president of the auxiliary of both TOMA and the AOA and as president of the hospital guild of the OMCT.

The couple settled in Fort Worth in 1946, just in time for Luibel to become a founding staff physician of the Fort Worth Osteopathic Hospital. He contributed a long career of distinguished service to his patients and to his adopted state of Texas. Luibel passed away at home in Fort Worth, aged 91, on June 7, 2003, a little more than a year after the death of his beloved Mary.

The TCOM Board meets with architect George Sowden (back to camera) in 1971. Left to right: Drs Sam Ganz, D.D. Beyer, Phil Russell, Carl Everett, Richard Stratton, Dene Wood (Secretary to Dr Hardt), Dr Hardt.

Luibel discussed the charter opportunity with his wife, Mary, one night and decided to proceed on his own. When they discussed who to approach for the other two required officer positions, Everett and Beyer leapt to mind. They were contacted the next day and promptly contributed $600 apiece, as did Luibel, to secure the charter. On June 15, 1966, Herman received the perpetual charter to operate a medical school in Fort Worth. The charter authorized the granting of DO degrees and other such scientific and honorary degrees as "may prove desirable," as well as allowing for nursing, medical technology and other associated schools. The charter was set up to permit from three to 20 directors. Luibel, Beyer and Everett were entered as the initial three directors: Luibel, president; Beyer, vice president; Everett, secretary-treasurer.

An osteopathic medical school for Texas existed on paper as a private, nonprofit corporation. All that remained was to make it real. The founders approached the TOMA House of Delegates seeking to expand the board. John Burnett, a general practitioner from Dallas, and Sam Ganz, also a general practitioner, of Corpus Christi, were added. The board held an all-day meeting at the Worth Hotel in downtown Fort Worth in September 1966 in which two key items were decided. The operational decision was to hire C. Ray Stokes to handle public relations and fundraising. They had interviewed him based on a recommendation from Tex Roberts of TOMA. Stokes' actual start would have to await sufficient funding. The strategic decision was, not knowing much about starting medical schools, to proceed slowly, take it one step at a time. The board met regularly thereafter.

Luibel applied to the AOA for a grant in 1967 and was soon the recipient of $30,000 in what he called "walking around money," funds

Danny D. Beyer

Gib Lewis likes to tell the story of getting his first political campaign rolling in Tarrant County in 1970 by speaking to the county's influential osteopathic association. Afterward, one of the DOs attending walked up to him, introduced himself as Danny Beyer, said he admired the young politician's forthright style and pressed a $100 bill into his hand. It was Lewis' first-ever campaign contribution. Lewis went on to win his election and eventually to become five-time speaker of the Texas House of Representatives and a steady friend to the Texas osteopathic profession. The Gibson D. Lewis Health Science Library that opened in 1986 on the campus of the University of North Texas Health Science Center is so-named to honor Lewis' unstinting help over many years.

It was just this ability to spot the potential in a person or the opportunity in a situation, together with a straight-shooting approach, that made Beyer a valuable part of the medical school's founding team. Beyer was also a long and trusted friend of George Luibel's going back to their student days together in Kirksville, both graduating in the class of 1936. However, Beyer, who had grown up and gone to college in Iowa, had gone on to establish a general practice in Oklahoma. He moved to Fort Worth with his wife, Helen, in 1945 and became involved in the start of the Fort Worth Osteopathic Hospital, serving as chairman of the General Practice Department and a member of the board of directors.

Beyer's brother Robert, also an osteopathic physician, joined him in Fort Worth. Danny's son Bryce and Robert's son David continued the line of Beyer DOs in the city, with Bryce having passed away in September 2010. Along with George Luibel and Carl Everett, Danny Beyer received an honorary Doctor of Humane Letters degree from TCOM in 1977 and the Founders' Medal in 1978. He died in August 1981, aged 71.

The Campus that Never Was

Bobby Gene Smith, DO, began a general practice in Arlington, Texas, the next large city east of Fort Worth, in the mid-1960s. He was active in the Texas Osteopathic Medical Association and by 1970 would be elected its president. Just prior to that, he was aware that the Texas College of Osteopathic Medicine still had not located a suitable permanent campus. He approached a patient of his, Arlington Mayor Tom Vandergriff, and quickly sold him on the desirability of bringing a medical college to the city.

Vandergriff went to his father, W. T. Vandergriff, who promptly, along with business partner Carlisle Cravens, offered a 50-acre tract in southeast Arlington to the school. TCOM's board promptly accepted, but opinion remained divided. The property, referred to as "the cornfield," was not yet the prime real estate it soon became. And a restriction that the property would return to the heirs if the land ever ceased to be used for educational purposes troubled George Luibel, who remained convinced that the school would thrive better if located in Fort Worth proper.

The classes that entered in 1970 and 1971 did so in temporary accommodations on the unfinished fifth floor of the Fort Worth Osteopathic Hospital and in a lightly refurbished bowling alley on Camp Bowie Boulevard. It became clear that sentiment ran strongly toward keeping TCOM in Fort Worth, even with the greater expense of having to purchase land for an urban campus. The generous grant of land in Arlington was returned to Vandergriff and Carlisle. In the meantime, however, carrying a $300,000 parcel of land on the books had been sufficient to persuade the American Osteopathic Association that TCOM was solvent and deserved accreditation.

that could be used to cover the general expenses of getting to the point of being able to raise money. By the 1968 TOMA convention in Houston, the school's directors were geared up for their first major fundraising effort. The board of directors had been expanded to include H. George Grainger of Tyler, John L. Witt of Groom, Glenn Kumm of Portland, Michael Calabrese of El Paso, James Fite of Bonham and Walters R. Russell of Dallas. All were osteopathic physicians and selected in some cases for their potential as medical school instructors (though Grainger was the only one to eventually teach at TCOM, commuting from Tyler three to four hours each way once a week). Businessman Stockseth was added as the realization had dawned that more experience in the commercial and political spheres would be useful for guiding the enterprise.

The process of asking for contributions always changes the equation. There were those who wondered aloud what these particular osteopathic practitioners knew about running a medical school (they only planned to start it, not run it). There were those who wondered aloud at the folly of putting money into an underfunded enterprise. There were even those who wondered aloud, why Fort Worth? Why not Houston? In the end, the Texas

Carl E. Everett

Carl Everett was born in 1914 in Mountain View, Arkansas. He took a degree from the University of Oklahoma and then received his DO degree from the Kansas City College of Osteopathic Medicine in 1939. He remained in Missouri for the next decade practicing general medicine.

Everett's friendship with Roy Fisher, founder of the Fort Worth Osteopathic Hospital, brought him and his young family to Fort Worth in 1949.

Tragedy struck in 1959 when his wife, Trudy, was killed in a car accident. It struck again a decade later when his second wife, Vyra, died from a heart attack. Two of his three sons died early in life.

In addition to his long association with the Texas College of Osteopathic Medicine that he helped found and for which he served as secretary-treasurer, Everett served a long term on the board of directors of the Osteopathic Medical Center of Texas and a year as chief of staff. With his tall, athletic build, Everett was an avid golfer. He was also active in the Masons and in Ridglea Presbyterian Church, becoming an ordained elder.

"Carl was always instrumental at bringing people together," recalled Tim Sullivan, son of Everett's longtime business partner, Dorothy Sullivan, whom Everett had first met when she was an administrator of the FWOH on Montgomery Street. Together they built and managed a series of nursing homes across North Texas. Most, innovatively, featured a clinic staffed daily and used for the care of both the home's residents and employees. At their Western Hills Nursing Home in Fort Worth, Everett and Sullivan partnered with three DOs and three MDs and opened it for TCOM students to use for their geriatric rotations. He added the MDs in part so that osteopathic students could gain experience working with MDs as colleagues, something he felt would be increasingly common over their careers.

Tragedy continued to follow Everett. His third wife, Mary Hope, died in 2007. He now resides in an elder-care living complex built down Summit Avenue from where the original Fort Worth Osteopathic Hospital that brought him to Fort Worth once stood.

osteopathic community came through with massive support — more than $100,000 in pledges reflecting 85 percent participation of the state's DOs. On top of this success, TOMA added a $20,000 grant-in-aid for the following year.

The new financial reserve allowed, and their busy practices necessitated, that the founding physicians turn over the process of moving the school to professional leadership and administration. Ray Stokes was finally brought on board as director of development, two-and-a-half years after he had been hired. He promptly rented a modest furnished office at 1500 West Fifth St., the college's first official space in May 1, 1969. No one knew at that point when or where the school's doors would open.

Stokes had just weeks to prepare for the 1969 TOMA convention in Dallas. There would be no repeat of the successful fundraising effort of the previous year. Instead, Stokes circulated a statement of the school's goals and began to gain visibility in the osteopathic community. By the following spring, for the Lubbock TOMA convention, fundraising resumed briskly. And Everett, as treasurer,

undertook some novel campaigns with good success. A letter campaign to AOA members outside Texas brought in $50,000, and a lunch for FWOH physicians at a Fort Worth country club raised $20,000 in the span of an hour. His "One Thousand Club," begun in November 1970, had 99 members by the following March, bringing $99,000 in contributions to the college-to-be.

In the meantime, Stokes had succeeded on the directive to find a dean for the school. Henry Hardt proved a fortuitous choice. He had retired after two decades as chair of the chemistry department at Texas Christian University across town and had been a leader in basic science higher education in the state. In February of 1970, to accommodate the staff now grown to three, TCOM moved its administrative offices into a small house at 3600 Mattison Ave., across the street from FWOH.

In the meantime, the school had secured temporary class-room space. In the winter of 1969-1970, Luibel was in his tenure as chairman of the board for FWOH. He came to see the unfinished fifth floor of the new hospital wing as a desirable temporary location

C. Ray Stokes

Ray Stokes was famously Texas College of Osteopathic Medicine's first employee (his personalized license plate proclaimed "TCOM-1"), with wife Edna its second. He also famously started out as a paperboy — er, scratch that, paper carrier/salesman — for the *Fort Worth Star-Telegram* (Stokes always credited the lessons of publisher Amon G. Carter for his sense of the dignity and importance of every job). He was well-known as a Sunday school teacher for more than 50 of his adult years and was legendary for the thousands of volunteer hours he devoted to the OMCT. And he was especially known as an enthusiastic ambassador for TCOM long beyond his "final" retirement in 1990 at age 78.

Stokes' "fame" derived from being a people person *par excellence*. With no children of their own, Ray and Edna "adopted" each incoming class at TCOM, willingly extending themselves on behalf of students, their families, the staff and faculty. He never forgot a name and greeted all with a two-handed handshake and a twinkle in his eye.

In 1943, at age 30, Stokes joined the Marines and was called "Grandpa" by the other members of his rifle platoon, all many years his junior. Before he embarked for Okinawa, the Marines noted his long career in the newspaper business and made him a combat reporter, or "combatless" reporter as Stokes would correct, given that he finally arrived overseas 10 days after the fighting had ended. Following the war, Stokes earned a degree

in journalism from TCU while at the same time running his own advertising agency.

In 1966, counting on his acquaintance with president Tex Roberts, Stokes applied for a job with the Texas Osteopathic Medical Association. He soon found himself instead interviewing with Drs Luibel, Beyer and Everett. What stood out for them was the great variety of work Stokes had undertaken — surely he could take on many roles in the topsy-turvy process of starting a new medical school — and the fact that some of his experience was in the realm of raising corporate donations. He was hired in the fall of 1966, conditional on sufficient funding being secured.

Stokes' employment finally took effect on April 15, 1969. He served as business manager and director of development, promptly opened TCOM's first office and hired his wife, Edna, as secretary and bookkeeper. Stokes was soon tasked with hiring Henry Hardt as the school's first dean and then, before Hardt took over faculty hiring, the school's first professor, Elizabeth (Libby) Harris. Stokes was indeed instrumental in raising money, using his close connection to the J. E. and L. E. Mabee Foundation of Tulsa, Oklahoma, to raise funds for the purchase of some of the properties acquired near the bowling alley. He also coordinated the effort to raise money from osteopathic physicians around the state.

Stokes retired in 1980 and soon un-retired. He went to work for TCOM librarian Craig Elam, raising funds for library acquisitions, taping oral histories of founders and osteopathic practitioners around the state and publishing a history of TCOM's first 20 years. In 1986, he received TCOM's Founders' Medal, a decade after he had received its Meritorious Service Award. For many years afterward, Stokes continued to attend TOMA meetings and to press fellow attendees to write those checks to TCOM and TOMA that kept osteopathic medicine moving forward. Stokes passed away May 11, 2007, aged 93.

▲

Phil R. Russell, DO, known far and wide as "Mr Osteopathy of Texas."

to get the medical school going until a permanent location could be secured. He floated the idea to the board but encountered opposition from Phil Russell, a key founder of the hospital whose influence over the board was at least equal to Luibel's. Russell was a backer of the medical school who wanted to keep the two institutions coordinated but separate, with the school taking its time to get properly set up rather than rush to open. Given Russell's misgivings, the board was not anxious to vote.

Everett scheduled a private meeting with Russell at his home to see if he could not persuade the man, revered as the elder statesman of Texas osteopathic medicine, to come around to support using the hospital's unused space. The appointed day turned out to be bitingly cold, record cold. All that Russell could do to warm his home, no better equipped against extreme cold than other Texas homes, availed little, and the two men sat in the parlor in their coats, able to see their breath frost up. They talked for five hours, at the end of which Russell pledged his support.

With little more than a year to go before the school's intended opening, Hardt began working on the tasks of hiring faculty and finalizing curriculum. Yet, no one he approached to serve on the full-time or volunteer faculty turned down the honor. Student applications were trickling in, too, which was good as the founders were wary of seeking applicants for a school not yet certain to open.

Then the unimaginable happened. In June, the *Star-Telegram* and the *Fort Worth Press*, combining a press release on the AOA having voted to grant pre-accreditation in May with the earlier suggestion that the school might be able to open as soon as the fall, printed stories that the new medical school would open that fall. Rather than panic, the TCOM board decided that with faculty recruitment and student applications proceeding nicely and with classroom space secured, it might make more sense to bend all effort toward making the dream come true sooner rather than try to put the PR genie back in the bottle. The planning horizon dropped from 15 months to just three.

Partitions were thrown up to create classrooms on the hospital's fifth floor and furnishings rounded up. The apartment atop the garage behind the house now home to TCOM's offices was rented to serve as the school's anatomy lab.

On October 1, 1970, the school received provisional accreditation for the school year from the AOA and on the same day opened its doors to 20 young students, the number allowed in the first year for AOA-approved medical schools, plus one special student, all seeking to become osteopathic physicians. Classes began the following Monday.

FWOH billed TCOM $40,000 for use of the fifth-floor space but graciously declined to collect. Because the space was barely sufficient for the one class, the challenge already existed where to fit two classes the following year. Stokes spent much of the year sleuthing locations in and around Fort Worth, only to find them priced out of the school's range or, in the case of idle federal property, claimed by government agencies. Then the Tavener Bowling Alley, only a couple of blocks down Camp Bowie Boulevard from the hospital and TCOM's office, came on the market.

▲
TOMA Director Tex Roberts, Sen. Tom Creighton, TOMA President Bobby Gene Smith, DO, Chairman George Luibel, Richard Hall, DO, and Rep. Cordell Hull, Jr, look on as Texas Gov. Preston Smith signs Senate Bill 160 into law in 1971.

Henry B. Hardt

Henry Hardt was a lifelong educator, having received bachelor's and master's degrees from Southwestern University in Georgetown, Texas, and taught at high schools in Bastrop and DeLeon. He returned to school, at Columbia University in New York City, earning another master's and a doctorate. He came back to Texas, teaching at a number of universities before joining the chemistry faculty at Texas Christian University in Fort Worth, eventually becoming department chair in 1946.

Ray Stokes set about finding a dean for the new school by inquiring of Jerome Moore, a dean he had known at TCU. Moore urged, "If you can get him, hire Henry Hardt." Hardt had retired from TCU a couple of years earlier. Stokes tracked him down teaching at a small college in East Texas. Hardt accepted the position of associate dean of Texas College of Osteopathic Medicine.

He was indeed the ideal man for the job, though not a DO. He had been the founding president of the Texas State Board of Examiners for the Basic Sciences and had been appointed to additional six-year terms by four different governors. For good measure, he had served two terms (1961-1963) as president of the National Collegiate Athletic Association. He took charge in October 1970 and immediately set about assembling the initial 10 members of the full-time faculty, along with 20 volunteer clinical instructors, and working with the curriculum committee. He also took an active role in interviewing student applicants.

Hardt's willingness to come on board lent the enterprise not just credibility but stature. He was known widely as a man of uncompromising high standards, a keen intellect with a bearing that immediately suggested grace and dignity. Hardt relinquished his position and retired when the first class graduated. The first issue of the college's yearbook, the 1974 *Speculum*, was dedicated to Hardt, "who led the college in its most difficult times ... and who always put the students first." He was awarded TCOM's Founders' Medal in 1980.

Marion E. Coy

Marion Coy is one of those rare men who enthusiastically work themselves out of a job. As the first president of the Texas College of Osteopathic Medicine, he realized that financial stability for the fledgling institution was priority number one. He attended every meeting of the Texas Higher Education Coordinating Board and invested considerable time in developing relationships with legislators. The payoff, in May 1975, was passage of Senate Bill 216 making TCOM a state-assisted medical school under the jurisdiction of the North Texas State University Board of Regents. This meant that NTSU president C. C. "Jitter" Nolen would automatically take over as TCOM president, too, and the presidency of TCOM would become a deanship.

Coy, a general practitioner and anesthesiologist from Jackson, Tennessee, was serving as president of the American Osteopathic Association in 1971 when fellow board member George Luibel approached him to serve as the first president of the recently opened TCOM. After a tour of the college, Coy agreed to the position. He had to divide his time starting in 1972, given his commitment to the AOA; he took on the role of president full-time beginning with the 1973 school year.

First orders of business were full accreditation by the AOA Bureau of Professional Education and full recognition by the Texas State Board of Medical Examiners. With these accomplished, Coy oversaw completion of two health care clinics, one urban and one rural. In 1974, he enjoyed the singular honor of presiding over TCOM's first graduation ceremony, of 18 doctors of osteopathic medicine.

Rather than step down from president to dean, in 1975 Coy returned to teaching as professor of osteopathic philosophy, principles and practices. He retired in 1983 after receiving TCOM's highest award, the Founders' Medal, in 1981 and after being named the school's first professor emeritus in 1982. He passed away November 1, 2001, aged 91.

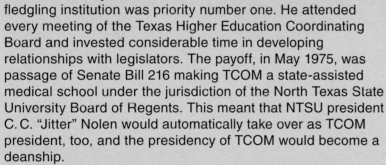

C. C. "Jitter" Nolen, president of North Texas State University, opened his campus in Denton to TCOM basic science classes.

The bowling alley was large enough to house faculty and administration offices and provide classroom and laboratory space for the second-year class and the 1971 incoming class of 32 regular and two special students. Luibel was quick to remind anyone who found the facility's former identity lowly that stately Southwestern Medical School in Dallas had begun in an old army barracks. Across the alley from the bowling alley, the school acquired a vacant lot, an apartment building with a seedy reputation, a liquor store and a "go-go" bar but lacked the funds for new building projects just yet. The bowling alley would not hold three classes, and the search was on again.

Luibel had received advice early in the process of starting TCOM that things would go much more swiftly if it were started privately and then taken over by the state rather than being founded under state auspices. The first state funding came on May 17, 1971, when Gov. Preston Smith signed Senate Bill 160. The legislation was basically the continuation of the out-of-state tuition program that had been started by Baum, now bumped up to $150,000 of direct support to TCOM. This amounted to more than $8,000 of support for each Texas-resident student.

The signing of the bill represented a coup for TOMA president Bobby Gene Smith and executive director Tex Roberts who, working with state Sen. Tom Creighton of Weatherford and Rep. Carlos Truan of Corpus Christi, had carried the ball on behalf of the school. It opened all administrative eyes to the bounty that could flow forth from well-crafted appeals to the state.

TCOM was also becoming an attractive partner for a university. Student numbers were growing with each class. The osteopathic profession would support the private school in the amount of more than $800,000. In addition, paid faculty members typically endorsed their paychecks back to the school. A grateful patient even made an individual gift of $70,000. With the help of U.S. Rep. Jim Wright and Sen. John Tower, federal money that would total more than $500,000 was beginning to arrive, in addition to the funds received from the state. More than $400,000 in private money — from the Amon G. Carter, Sid W. Richardson and J. E. and L. E. Mabee foundations — would be received. Some of these funds had been put to use to acquire an entire city block, plus some additional properties, in the desirable area between the school's Administration Building and the Fort Worth Osteopathic Hospital.

Despite the appeal of the new school for a university partner, the two Fort Worth universities — Texas Christian and Texas Wesleyan

In May 1975, Gov. Dolph Briscoe signs the law taking TCOM from private to publicly assisted. Looking on are (l-r) Rep. Gib Lewis, TCOM President Marion Coy, TOMA President Bobby Gene Smith, Carl Everett, George Luibel, Sen. Betty Andujar, D.D. Beyer, Michael Calabrese, TOMA Director Tex Roberts, Robert Nobles and John Burnett.

— were private. The nearby University of Texas at Arlington showed no interest in partnering. However, North Texas State University in Denton (since 1988 the University of North Texas) did show interest in forming a relationship. TCOM faculty member Robert Nobles and another Denton osteopathic physician, Art Wiley, began casual talks with Dr J. K. G. "Gwynn" Silvey, distinguished professor of biological sciences at NTSU, resulting in Silvey being invited to speak at the 1971 AOA convention in Hawaii. In Hawaii, George Luibel and others joined the discussion. On his return to Texas, Silvey phoned NTSU President C. C. Nolen and inquired whether he would like a medical school as part of the university. Nolen, newly inaugurated that August, was certainly ready to discuss the possibility. He got Dr Gus Ferré, academic vice president, involved as well.

By January, it was worked out that beginning in the fall TCOM's basic science courses would be taught at NTSU in Denton with students being bused up to Denton for classes. NTSU made the offer attractive: the cost to TCOM to teach the core science curriculum to each student would be $1,000 for the school year. For the new school year, given this change, the name of the bowling alley was changed from TCOM Basic Science Building to the Administration Building but continued always to be known as "the bowling alley." By the following school year, 1973, the state would cover the entire cost of instruction at NTSU for TCOM students.

In spring of 1972, before the shuttles to Denton got underway, TCOM hired its first president, Marion E. Coy, of Tennessee. Coy, who served only as dean until his term as president of the AOA was completed a few months later, was aware of and receptive to the discussion with NTSU, but a higher early priority was to shore up the school's finances and its relations with the state's osteopathic practitioners. He asked Fort Worth general practitioner Clifford

Dickey, DO, to lead a support group, the Friends of TCOM. What some were beginning to call a period of divisiveness over the school was more accurately a period of rumor and misconception in the osteopathic community regarding accreditation and other issues. The series of dinner meetings and other communications established by Coy and Dickey went a long way toward keeping the osteopathic community abreast of changes and intentions at TCOM.

As TCOM began to ponder its first graduation, an inspection team from the Texas State Board of Medical Examiners, in December 1973, recommended full recognition of the school to their board, making the graduates eligible to take the state licensure examination. The following month, an inspection team from the AOA Bureau of Professional Education recommended the college for full recognition. In a word, TCOM was legit.

That same spring, Coy was traveling the state and devoting much more of his attention to the matter of a merger with NTSU. Early in 1975, state Rep. Gib Lewis and Sen. Betty Andujar, whose husband was a supportive Fort Worth MD, ushered a bill through the Texas legislature that provided for TCOM to become a state-supported institution operating separate from NTSU but under jurisdiction of its president and board of regents. Andujar, in particular, displayed a lot of courage as her husband came under attack from his peers. She even had to defeat a counter-proposal from the MD community to form an MD school in association with Texas Woman's University in Denton.

When Senate Bill 216 was signed into law that May by Gov. Dolph Briscoe, TCOM's board ceased to exist. Founders Luibel, Beyer and Everett, all enthusiastic backers of the move to state support, surrendered their roles in the governance of the school.

Coy's position as president no longer existed. He chose to stay on the faculty rather than accept the deanship but spent the following year consulting to NTSU President Nolen. Henry Hardt had retired, as he had always planned, the year before with the graduation of the school's first class. The old guard exited with TCOM's days as its own private entity having come to a satisfactory and all-around successful conclusion, its future pretty much assured. ▪

People DO Change Their Minds

▲
Gwynn Silvey speaks at a general-practice seminar in Hawaii, 1981

North Texas State's distinguished Professor of Biology Gwynn Silvey may have set in motion the union between the public university and the private medical college, but his esteem for the osteopathic profession was news to one of his former students.

"In 1981, I was asked to arrange speakers for the general-practice seminar following the American Osteopathic Convention in Hawaii," recalls Eugene Zachary, DO. "I was told that Dr Gwynn Silvey of North Texas State University was available to speak. I said there must be some mistake, but, no, I was told, he had addressed the convention 10 years earlier and been very well-received."

Zachary went on to serve as dean of the Texas College of Osteopathic Medicine from 1984 to 1990. What had given him pause was remembering his student experiences from the 1950s ... at NTSU ... under Dr Silvey. "When I asked Dr Silvey if he would write a letter of recommendation for me to the Kansas City College of Osteopathy and Surgery where I wanted to study, he implored me not to throw my life away by associating with a cult that was not an acceptable part of the medical profession. I was crushed. He had been such an outstanding professor, I really wanted his good opinion. I went on to Kansas City without his blessing."

When Silvey enthusiastically accepted the speaking invitation, Zachary felt "flabbergasted." "We had time to visit in Hawaii, and he was unreservedly supportive of my profession. He brought his wife along, and mine was there. We all became good friends. But I never could bring myself to ask him what had turned his opinion so completely around. It was enough to finally have his good opinion."

▲
Friends of TCOM, March 1973: Edward T. Newell, Clifford E. Dickey and Marion E. Coy

The Graduating Class of 1974

Name	Hometown	College
Weldon E. Bond	Gatesville	North Texas State
Robert J. Breckenridge	Big Spring	Texas Tech
Kenneth J. Brock	Oklahoma City, Okla.	Central State, Okla.
Jobey D. Claborn	Friona	Southwestern State, Okla.
Nelda D. Cunniff, RN	Fort Worth	Texas Woman's
Ronald L. Daniels	Fort Worth	Texas Wesleyan
Gilbert E. Greene	Sweetwater	Sul Ross
Robert G. Holston	Borger	West Texas State
Shelley M. Howell	Temple	Southwestern U
Sterling F. Lewis	New Market, Md.	Baylor
Ronald Paul Livingston	Comanche	Tarleton State
Terry L. Parvin	Austin	Tarleton State
Jesse R. Ramsey	Fort Worth	Texas Wesleyan
David A. Ray	Bridgeport	U Houston, Wesleyan
John L. Sessions	Arlington	UT Arlington
Ronald D. Sherbert	Van	Stephen F. Austin
John H. Williams	Arlington	UT Arlington
Thomas David Wiman	Snyder	Hardin-Simmons

The year 1974 saw 593 new doctors of osteopathic medicine graduated from the country's seven osteopathic colleges, 45 of them from Texas. While 16 Texans were graduated in Texas, 23 were graduated from the two schools in Missouri. Jobey Claborn had been the first student enrolled in TCOM, and, by alphabetical luck, Weldon Bond became the first DO graduated in Texas.

TCOM faculty, staff and well-wishers gather for cake on the day the school opened, October 1, 1970.

The First 20 Years

The definitive account of the school's early history is to be found in *Texas College of Osteopathic Medicine: The First Twenty Years* by C. Ray Stokes and Judy Alter. The book is no longer in print but can be found in most osteopathic libraries.

1970-71 Faculty

Joel Alter, DO	Surgery-Anatomy
Jack W. Banister, PhD	Biochemistry, Cell Physiology, Microbiology
Raymond E. Beck, DO	Radiology
Edward A. Becka, DO	ENT
Gerald D. Bennett, DO	Pathology-Histology
Catherine K. Carlton, DO	Osteopathic Theory and Technique, History of Medicine
Virginia P. Ellis, DO	History of Medicine
Charles D. Farrow, DO	Surgery
Roy B. Fisher, DO	Surgery
Tom M. Graham, PhD	Cell Physiology
H. George Grainger, DO	Osteopathic Theory and Technique
Henry B. Hardt, PhD	Associate Dean
Elizabeth F. Harris, PhD	Embryology, Microbiology
Constance I. Jenkins, DO	Cell Physiology
William R. Jenkins, DO	Surgery-Anatomy
John C. Kemplin, DO	Radiology
George J. Luibel, DO	Osteopathic Theory and Technique, History of Medicine
Robert H. Nobles, DO	Physical Diagnosis
George F. Pease, DO	Surgery-Anatomy
Charles J. Rudolph, Jr, PhD	Biochemistry
Diana Rudolph, MA	Biochemistry
Phil R. Russell, DO	History of Medicine
Mary Lu Schunder, MA*	Gross Anatomy
Myron G. Skinner, DO	Pathology-Histology
Joan Swaim, MLS	Librarian
Tom W. Whittle, DO	Medical Psychology

* Dr Schunder received her PhD in 1977

TCOM's founding basic science faculty, 1970. Front row (l-r): Mary Lu Schunder, anatomy; Elizabeth "Libby" Harris, microbiology; Tom Graham, cell physiology. Back row: Dean Henry Hardt; Charles Rudolph, biochemistry; Jack Banister, biochemistry and cell physiology.

The Osteopathic Medical Center of Texas A history of TCOM is not complete without mention of the "O."

Roy Fisher, DO, founder of FWOH, had a faculty appointment in surgery at TCOM.

The Fort Worth Osteopathic Hospital opened its doors in the downstairs of the Roy Fisher home, the former Duringer house, at 1402 Summit Ave. The impetus for its establishment came from several different influencing circumstances. First, an osteopathic hospital had opened in a private house in Amarillo and become self-supporting. By 1946, it was reopening in larger, custom-built quarters. Second, the Hill-Burton Act had passed Congress, providing federal funds to match state and local funds with the goal of achieving four-and-a-half hospital beds per thousand population in communities across the nation. And, third, while it is practical for primary care practitioners to work from a private office, surgeons and other providers of tertiary care need the resources of a hospital. By war's end, Fort Worth had a critical mass of osteopathic surgeons and specialists, but they were being denied privileges in the city's existing hospitals.

Surgeon Roy B. Fisher took the lead. In January 1947, the group began an ambitious $200,000 fundraising campaign. Shares were sold for $50 each to raise operating capital from a distinguished group of doctors of osteopathy, including Fisher's brother, Raymond, and future Texas College of Osteopathic Medicine founders George Luibel and D.D. Beyer. Virgil L. Jennings was elected president. Other participants included Phil and Roy Russell, Edward LaCroix, L. V. Parker, Catherine K. Carlton, R. W. Briscoe, Percy Hatcher, A. L. Fountain, Helene R. Kenney, M. Sloan Miller, Hugo J. Ranelle, Lester Hamilton, Arthur Clinch, Horace M. Walker and J. R. Thompson.

The enterprise succeeded, quickly expanding from two to 10 beds and including an operating room and a nursery. Soon the Fisher family had to buy another house and move out altogether so that the upstairs could be put in service as well. It was understood from the beginning that the use of a private home was a temporary measure, a stopgap until a much larger modern hospital could be built. A committee was formed — Roy Fisher, Jennings, Beyer and Miller — to work with Phil Russell, who had the connections to the city's leading philanthropists, to locate funding, identify a site, secure architectural services and find contractors — all it would take to make the dream a reality.

Russell donated a small parcel of land that he owned on the western side of town, given to him previously by friend and patient Amon G. Carter, by then the well-to-do publisher of the city's main newspaper. Carter got involved and pledged to loan the shareholders of Fort Worth "O" an amount equal to the funds they could raise. Then he would call on his friend (and also Russell's patient and friend) oil magnate Sid Richardson to split the cost of furnishing the new facility. This is how it proceeded, apart from the minor hurdle that Richardson complained by phone to Russell that his share for

Fort Worth Osteopathic Hospital began in 1946 in the ground floor of the Fishers' home, the former Duringer home, on Summit Avenue. The family lived upstairs but soon moved to a new home as the hospital flourished.

Fort Worth Osteopathic Hospital moved to its permanent location on Montgomery Street in 1956. In 1968, a new wing added 80 beds, more than doubling the size of the hospital and adding an unfurnished fifth floor that would house TCOM in its first year.

furnishing the building came to half again more than Carter had led him to expect. Russell teased his friend, "When you get out here this afternoon, I'll give you my check for the difference, because I know you can't afford it." "You go to hell," Richardson howled in reply, but he brought along his check for the full amount. On January 1, 1950, the new 26-bed Fort Worth Osteopathic Hospital opened at 3705 Camp Bowie Blvd.

Jennings and Russell stated their vision very clearly: "While doctors have claimed they made hospitals, the facts are hospitals 'made' doctors." So, they instituted a ceiling on patient charges, and the doctors would contribute a portion of their fees to the hospital expansion fund. It was to be an "open-staff" hospital, available to all physicians of the community. As Phil Russell said at the dedication, "It has been our dream to build a nonprofit hospital and to open and dedicate it to the people. We do not build it for any doctor."

This facility, too, was but a stopgap. Russell's idea was to start small and grow rationally. Carter continually challenged him to think bigger. No sooner was this facility up and running than work started on a new, grander hospital. Russell took Carter to scout side-by-side plots on a hilltop only half-a-dozen blocks from the new facility. Carter marveled at the panoramic view of downtown and wondered aloud how he had never visited the locale before. As Russell began to gesture where the hospital could be situated, Carter told him to put his arm down, "Somebody'll figure we're interested in buying the property and the price will go

sky high. Just buy it." When Russell averred he had not the means, Carter bought it.

Carter was instrumental in another important way. He had been successful in getting Methodist Hospital funded many years earlier but quit its board in disgust when the administration refused to relent on allowing service privileges to osteopathic physicians. He stipulated that FWOH and any other hospital he might ever participate in would be chartered to offer privileges to any qualified physician, DO or MD.

The new state-of-the-art, 78-bed facility opened July 29, 1956, at 1000 Montgomery St. A year earlier, as Russell watched the construction proceed, he thought of the constant admonishments of Carter, who had just recently passed away, to think bigger. Russell went to the master contractor and told him to go ahead and add an unfurnished fourth floor; he would find a way to fund it. Another planned wing added 80 more beds and, providentially, an unfinished fifth floor that would soon enable the fledgling TCOM to open its doors when it suddenly had to. It would be completed in 1968.

The hospital "for the people" prospered, especially after becoming the primary teaching hospital for TCOM in 1975. By 1981, it had completed an $8 millon expansion to accommodate new emergency, labor and delivery, radiology and outpatient departments and changed its name to the Fort Worth Osteopathic Medical Center. The latest in biomedical technology followed: cardiac telemetry, hemodialysis, stress testing, a computed tomography (CT) full-body scanner. By 1986, the hospital had grown to 265 beds, making it the largest osteopathic hospital in Texas.

In 1989, the "Osteopathic Medical Center of Texas" (OMCT, for short) was deemed a designation more befitting the hospital's regional status. Eventually, 11 neighborhood clinics were established to extend the reach of its family medicine and rural health services. It continued providing valuable service to the community and to osteopathic students during the 1990s, expanding its corporate umbrella beyond the hospital to independent home care, skilled nursing, fitness and child-development services. A 1989 joint venture with TCOM introduced hyperbaric medicine to North Texas, growing by 1993 into the Hyperbaric Oxygen/Wound Treatment Center, the county's only multi-place chamber.

All seemed to be going well until, after the millennium, economics turned hard. Following three money-losing years, the OMCT closed its doors on very short notice, October 8, 2004, leaving 1,000 employees, 300 physicians and 60 interns and residents scrambling.

The reasons for the collapse were even more varied than the rationales for founding it in the first place. A post-mortem in the *Journal of the American Osteopathic Association* pinpointed several factors — from increased patient costs inherent in the more-hands-on nature of osteopathic care to urgently needed renovations estimated at $16.5 million, cost restructuring occasioned by managed care, all the way to "town-gown" tensions between the medical school and the hospital. But the overarching reason cited was that at a time when the osteopathic profession had gained respect and full parity in the medical world, the compelling need for independent osteopathic hospitals was gone. In blunt terms, the OMCT had become victim to osteopathic success.

Biomedical Communications

Tarrant County Junior College in Fort Worth had earned a national reputation in the 1970s for its cutting-edge media center. Marion Coy, always a forward-looking man, decided to pay a visit. He arranged a tour of the center with its young director, Ken Coffelt. He then asked Coffelt to come take a look at what they were trying to set up at the bowling alley.

When Coffelt arrived, Coy showed him the space set aside for the instructional media department. Then he asked point-blank whether Coffelt would like to come to work for TCOM and build the department. As it turned out, Coffelt's undergraduate degree was in biology. That and the chance to build a second center to surpass his first one convinced Coffelt to start work at TCOM, January 1974.

As director of Biomedical Communications, Coffelt (on the right, with Coy, above) built a department that has offered major advantages to faculty for curriculum development and media access and to students for media-aided learning. The department, in 1986, settled into Med Ed 3, where it has over the years provided a wide range of services, including taping and filming, audio recording, medical illustration, even bioelectronics and repair of biomedical equipment.

Coffelt retired in 1997. Today, the department is headed by Robert Wright and is organized along with Information Technology Services, the Lewis Library and Records Management under the office of Vice Provost Renee Drabier, PhD.

Rates Increased at Fort Worth Osteopathic Hospital in 1946

Hospital Beds and Care, per day	from $5 to $6
Obstetrical Cases	
Delivery Room	from $7.50 to $10
Labor and Delivery	$7.50
Anesthesia, if used	$7.50 and up
Major Surgery	
Operating Room	$10
Anesthesia, local or general	$7.50 and up
Tonsil and Adenoid Operations	
Special Operating Room	$7.50 plus day's hospitalization and anesthesia, if used

HUMBLE BEGINNINGS

A Top-Hat Education on a Shoestring Budget

By Judy Alter

Humble beginnings is the only way to describe the first years of the Texas College of Osteopathic Medicine. And those beginnings led to stories that make many of us nostalgic, others a bit uptight. Some may have become embellished over the years or may even be a bit apocryphal. But they deserve to be told. To me, it's one of the marvels that this great school grew out of such humble beginnings.

In spite of the fact that an osteopathic school had long been a gleam in the eye of Dr George Luibel, it was April 1969 before Ray Stokes became the first and only paid staff member of TCOM. He worked out of the den at his home and soon hired his wife, Edna, for $1.75/hour. Years later, she would recall that the founders handed her a brown envelope with some bank statements, cancelled checks and a checkbook. They told her to set up the books, and she did, having previously worked as a bookkeeper. The operation moved to a small office at 1500 W. Fifth St., rented furnished for $110 a month, and then to a house at 3600 Mattison Ave., across from Fort Worth Osteopathic Hospital, the largest osteopathic hospital in the state. Edna Stokes thought she was probably the only bookkeeper who had to clean a bathtub, but since the office was in a house, there was a bathtub — and it had to be cleaned. No maid service. Because of the tight budget, she brought a coffeepot and a pencil sharpener from home — and used to bring the pencils, too.

Stokes did a little bit of everything. Tommy Hawkes, TCOM photographer since 1977, used to tell Stokes he was really the first photographer for the school. Stokes worked on recruiting faculty, recruiting students and anything else that needed to be done. His major challenge was to promote the college in the community, and he met that challenge ably. Dr Luibel put Stokes to work scouting possible campus locations and organizing fundraising campaigns.

Then Luibel said to him, "Hire us a dean."

Stokes, a graduate of Texas Christian University, went to Dean Jerome Moore there, and he recommended Dr Henry Hardt, a retired chemistry professor and chair of that department. Dr Hardt described himself as ideally suited to helping establish a medical school, having "a tough body and brain that was slow and stubborn, which required all the help available for such service to humanity." In truth, he was an amazing man, multilingual though he spoke English with a slight accent from his native tongue of German, possessed of a corny, wry sense of humor that was always spot on and a compassionate disposition that can only be described as sweet yet tough. Dr Elizabeth Harris, known to all as Libby, the first faculty

TCOM — The Greatest Show on Earth, a Sandra Stober illustration from the 1975 *Speculum* depicts Luibel, Coy and Newell kicking it up for an audience of Tuffies.

member hired as professor of microbiology, later said that Drs Hardt and Luibel were the two wisest men she ever knew. Of Hardt, she also said he was a hard-headed German but "had a dignity and grace that inspired us all."

Dr Hardt's job was to recruit both faculty and students, 20 students who would face an untried faculty with an untried curriculum and a questionable future. What if the school closed after the first or second year? Hardt did not solicit students, following Luibel's belief that if the college effort failed, they would not want to be in the embarrassing position of having solicited students to attend a doomed educational program. Potential students learned of the program by word of mouth, mainly in physicians' offices or by way of pharmaceutical representatives. Applicants would have to understand that the school might not last more than a year, but in that case every effort would be made to find each student a place at another osteopathic college. Applications were received as early as February 1970, although no opening date had been announced.

In sharp contrast to today's TCOM students, who are provided their own laptop computers, in the bowling-alley days, medical students were expected to provide even their own microscopes. Many of the photos included throughout show other aspects of change over our 40 years.

Catherine Carlton, DO, taught osteopathic theory and technique and history of medicine.

Hardt, hired in early 1969, wanted at least a year of planning as he began to recruit faculty, a task made easier by his own academic prestige. He spoke of his "audacity" in hiring faculty for a school that did not exist. No one he asked refused the challenge: Dr Tom Graham joined as physiologist; Dr Russ Jenkins, surgery; Dr Charles Rudolph, biochemist; Rudolph's wife, Diana, who held an MS in chemistry, became an assistant to the faculty. Mary Lu Schunder, anatomist, inquired about a position because of Hardt; she had studied under him at TCU and thought his professional reputation gave credibility to the school that still existed only on paper. Harris reports that they were delighted to see her, because finding someone to teach gross anatomy was difficult. At the time, Schunder had a master's degree; her doctorate would come in a few years. Hardt had sent her to Southwestern to ask the chairman about securing cadavers. "You can't just requisition them," he told her. Schunder, along with George Pease, another anatomy professor, would have to become members of the Anatomical Board of the University of Texas Medical Branch at Galveston. The law was written when the Galveston branch was the only medical school in the state, but Dr Luibel asked his lawyer, Abe Herman, to check the law for him.

Herman had written the charter that was submitted to the state legislature. It was ideal, Harris says, because it said that TCOM could grant all degrees it deemed appropriate in addition to the DO degree. Thus, it laid the foundation for the School of Public Health, a physician assistant program and other schools to come under the umbrella of the University of North Texas Health Science Center. Once again, Dr Luibel and his colleagues planned for all obstacles and approached them with insight and wisdom.

Other members of the new faculty were Drs Jack Banister (microbiology and biochemistry) and Joel Alter (anatomy-surgery) with Joan Hewatt Swaim as librarian. Harris was appointed chair of the curriculum committee, with Dr Gerald Bennett, a pathologist, and Dr John Kemplin, a radiologist, as members. The students also benefited from visiting lecturers such as osteopathic physicians Chet Godel, Mel Johnson and Ellis Mumtaz, who gave freely of their time.

The school still had no quarters, and the suggestion was made that the unused fifth-floor shell of the hospital could be converted to classrooms and laboratories. Dr Phil Russell, called "Mr Osteopathy of Texas" by many, and the man who had originally gotten the land for the hospital, opposed having the college in hospital quarters, and the TCOM board knew the hospital board would go whichever way Russell wanted. Carl Everett volunteered to go talk to Russell; he went to Russell's home on a Sunday when a "blue norther" had come through, and they sat in the cold front room for five hours, Everett keeping his overcoat on the whole time. Finally Russell agreed, and from that moment on it became his idea to put the college on the fifth floor.

By the time AOA pre-accreditation came in late July, an opening of October 1 had been announced. Luibel later said they were tricked into that because the newspapers publicized the date before the administration had actually decided on it. Among the things to be hastily done: remodel the fifth floor. Stokes recalled putting up partitions to make a classroom, a laboratory, a student lounge and a few faculty offices. Chairs, desks, tables were assembled wherever they could be found cheaply — mostly from the Federal Surplus Agency. TCU provided lab equipment, almost as a gift.

Osteopathic pediatrician Virginia Ellis lectures in the bowling alley as Tuffy the skeleton looks on.

The biochemistry stockroom begins to take shape on the fifth floor of the FWOH, home to TCOM only for the 1970-71 school year. The available unused space was large enough only for the college's entering class.

TCOM's 1970-71 offices on Mattison Avenue across from the FWOH housed Hardt, the Stokes and Schunder. The anatomy lab occupied the garage apartment.

Left: Interior view of the anatomy lab.

Several faculty members moved to small offices on the fifth floor. Schunder stayed in the little house, to be close to the anatomy lab. It was in the upstairs garage apartment behind the house, because Dr Russell, rightly, would not allow cadavers in the hospital (probably state law also forbade it). Schunder liked to joke that the size of the garage apartment determined the size of the school's first class —

there was room for four tables, five students to a table. (In fact, a first-year class size of 20 was an AOA requirement.)

Twenty students appeared on October 1, plus one special student — George Jurek, a dentist whom Hardt accepted because of his knowledge of anatomy. He would assist in teaching anatomy classes. Nineteen men and one woman, Nelda Cunniff, risk-takers all. Their average age was 27, older than most entering medical students. They were from many other professions, including at least one pharmacist and one former naval officer. Four years later, 18 of those students would graduate; one repeated the first year and graduated in the next class, one withdrew, and the special student shortly returned to dentistry.

In those four years, the students pioneered in countless ways. Dr Hardt told both faculty and students, "Few have the opportunity to found a medical school." The class bonded quickly into one group. Not only were students close to each other, but wives and children became part of the cohesiveness. They pitched in to carry furniture from behind the house on Mattison Avenue to the fifth floor. Students and their wives spent a week painting and decorating the

Tavener's Bowling Alley is shown shortly after its conversion to an osteopathic medical school in the fall of 1971. For the first year, it was known as the Basic Science Building, afterward as the Administration Building.

Top right: The library in the bowling alley.

Right: Members of the Texas Higher Education Coordinating Board inspect the gross anatomy lab in 1971.

lounge. "They were," said Schunder, "literally 24-hour students. They truly helped build the college."

There were donated items everywhere — a faculty member gave "early attic" furniture for the ladies lounge, which students called "Nelda's lounge" in tribute to the lone woman in their midst. The reception area was decorated with paintings by Vyra Everett, wife of founder Carl Everett.

Physicians cleared their office shelves to donate to the library, though many of the books were old medical texts. Only about 30 were new. Someone shelved the books before Swaim arrived, a gesture she appreciated, but she said, "Of course, I had to take them off the shelves and re-shelve them in order." When she toured area medical libraries and mentioned that she had not yet been able to purchase such essential works as *Index Medicus,* a donation was forthcoming; she carried the books from her car to the fifth floor, a few at a time.

Dr David Ray (a member of the first class) still laughs over the night someone broke into the anatomy lab — nothing was stolen, but one of the body bags was opened. Ray said the robbery apparently ended right then, and the would-be burglars left rather rapidly. Then there's the story about dressing a skeleton in a lab coat, hat and shoes so students could walk it across the street to the anatomy lab. Who knows if it really happened?

Faculty taught outside their area of specialization. When asked what she wanted to teach, pediatrician Dr Virginia Ellis blurted, "Not pediatrics." She taught history of medicine. One day, she found Libby

Harris in her office surrounded by big fat textbooks and scribbling furiously. "What in the world are you doing?" she asked. Harris replied, "Well, I've got to teach a class in pathology, and there's no one else to do it, so I'm going to do it." The next day, Harris, pregnant and due at the time, sat on a concrete foundation left in the lecture hall and showed slides sitting down. Later that afternoon, she delivered a daughter. Her recovery room turned out to be on the fifth floor of FWOH, now converted back to hospital rooms, but in space she had once occupied as an office.

At the end of the first year, faculty and students were able to look back and agree that they worked hard, harder than ever in their lives for most of them, but it was a year of accomplishment, and all felt good about it. It was, in the general opinion, an important phase of life. Of course there were dissatisfactions, questions about the education they were getting, concerns about the future of the school. One student suggested that medical students tend to stay a bit dissatisfied, explaining that the grind of school makes it easy for doubt and stress to arise.

An interesting statistic about that first class: most students were married, and if memory serves, four of those marriages dissolved upon graduation. No one has yet reached any conclusion about that, but I remember meeting with student wives that first year and suggesting they look around, because one out of four of them wouldn't be there in a few years.

The school did indeed open again in 1971, welcoming a class of 32 plus two special students, 25 of whom would graduate four years later (that high attrition rate owes mostly, in various ways, to administration apprehension over state and AOA accreditation). By then, the school had rented an old bowling alley across the street, and several classrooms and labs, including anatomy, were moved to the hastily converted bowling alley, so hastily converted that President Coy's office in the former bar still had red carpet on the walls! A general surgeon bought 30 gallons of paint and rounded up faculty and students for a weekend of painting and refurbishing — those were indeed do-it-yourself days.

Fort Worth surgeon Sam Buchanan, DO, was one of those in that class, and he has vivid memories of both his application process and various incidents at the school. Buchanan was a third-year student at TCU in the pre-med program run by Willis G. Hewatt, PhD, whose reputation was outstanding. No one he had ever recommended to a medical school had been turned down. Buchanan would enter medical school at the end of his junior year, instead of completing his fourth year. At the end of his first year of medical school, he would get his undergraduate degree. The practice was common in those years.

As Buchanan tells the story, his father was a friend of George Luibel, and when Sam announced he was going to apply to the state school in Galveston, his father said, "You better go talk to Dr Luibel first." So he did. Luibel made quite a positive impression on young Buchanan, which, together with his preference to stay in Fort Worth, was enough to convince him to choose TCOM.

So the pre-med student went back to Hewatt and asked for a letter to TCOM. Hewatt began to lecture, pointing his finger in Sam's face and declaring he would never write such a letter, ending with "They're quacks!" Buchanan was taken aback — to him, doctors were doctors; he had no idea there were any differences, much less that someone he revered would hold his choice of osteopathic medicine disreputable. Defeated, he went the next day to talk to Luibel and explain he would not be attending the school. He went to the library, where Swaim happened to be sitting at one of the tables.

▶

Top: For seven years beginning in the fall of 1971, students shuttled by bus between the Denton and Fort Worth campuses for basic science classes.

Middle: The Biology Building on the North Texas State campus in 1973.

Bottom: TCOM Class at NTSU.

"Young man," she asked, "are you going to come to school here?"

Glumly, he replied that he had intended to but his pre-med advisor at TCU refused to write him a letter of recommendation because he believed the school was full of quacks. To his astonishment, she replied, "Daddy said that? I'll just go talk to him tonight. This is a good school."

He had no idea that Swaim was Hewatt's daughter, but, desperate not to ruin his good record at TCU, he asked her not to intervene. The next day, Hewatt called him into his office, and Buchanan thought his career as a student was over. Instead, Hewatt said, "Joanie came to see me last night ... I'll write your letter." Swaim does not quite remember the story, but then she didn't have as much on the line.

Buchanan said he was in a group that went to pick up cadavers in Dallas in a U Haul. They drove back very cautiously — they sure didn't want to be pulled over — and just as carefully they unloaded the cadavers into the bowling alley anatomy lab (the building was never called anything else in spite of the prominent sign on the front that proclaimed "Texas College of Osteopathic Medicine").

The presence of practicing surgeons such as Joel Alter and Russ Jenkins in the classroom demonstrates what Harris calls one of the great advantages of the first two years. "The students had a unique, wonderful experience because we were across the street from a hospital." Once, Gerald Bennett, the pathologist, called her from his lab at the hospital while she was teaching immunology. He had some unusual slides, so she took her class to his lab, and he showed them the slides. "You don't get to do that anymore," she noted.

She also pointed out that allopathic physicians (that is, MDs) were generous with their time and expertise. An expert in parasitic microbiology from Southwestern Medical School in Dallas lectured frequently, giving students not arcane knowledge but what they needed to know to practice medicine — like information about pinworms. Once, he discussed the case of a man losing his sight in one eye; it was discovered that the man had a parasitic tapeworm in his eye. The microbiologist showed a film of the surgery to remove the tapeworm to first-year students in class. Harris didn't comment about the students' reaction but said she almost had to turn her own head away.

▲ Robert Kaman lectures to his biochemistry class in the bowling alley. An overhead projector and screen stand ready for use.

That close physical proximity — the fifth-floor quarters, the bowling alley, the garage anatomy lab and the hospital — did indeed give students a unique experience. But during the spring of 1973, TCOM administrators negotiated an affiliation with North Texas State University (now the University of North Texas) whereby TCOM students would study the basic sciences on the Denton campus. TCOM began to run buses back and forth to Denton, effectively splitting the student body. Faculty also made the commute to Denton. (It would be several years yet before TCOM went under the umbrella of UNT and became the University of North Texas Health Science Center, with its diverse programs.) In addition, some TCOM administrative offices moved to space in a local bank building. The school was growing, and the campus was fragmenting, though it would reunite with the construction of Medical Education Building 2 (commonly called Med Ed 2) in the early 1980s. The building, containing labs, classrooms, clinics and offices, brought all the students back together on the Fort Worth campus. And by 1990, there were 400 students enrolled, 20 times more students in 20 years!

The days of humble beginnings were long gone. ▧

TEACHING TALES

Memorable scenes from the classrooms

Looking out on today's students across the various schools of the Health Science Center, one is struck by the earnest, dedicated, even, focused and serious approach they take to their educations and careers. It is quite difficult to conceive that their predecessors of a couple of generations harbored a streak of mischief ready to burst at any moment like an aneurysm of mirth and mayhem.

What could account for this discrepancy? Certainly much ink has poured forth on the subject of the Sixties generation, whose numbers questioned everything "put on their plates," versus more recent "go with the flow" generations.

Maybe it had to do with attending classes in a hastily converted bowling alley versus the state-of-the-art lecture halls and labs now available, in close-knit classes of 20- or 30-something rather than one 100-something.

Perhaps the quality of student in the early classes was not on par with today's crop; yet, they now are wrapping up exceptional careers, those early students. No question the quality of the faculty was quite a bit more uneven in the early days. Beyond the few top-talent visionaries who found themselves at a point in their careers where they could afford to lend themselves to building a medical school for

The Winnebago Mobile Medical Clinic was diagnosed as hyper-mobile (it swayed side to side) and non-compliant (it required major effort to bring to a stop). Student Nelda Cunniff listens as Ed Newell and Virginia Ellis discuss the day's medical screening foray.

the future, there was whoever could be attracted to an iffy situation and plugged in on short notice on a volunteer basis, as there was no budget for faculty salaries. The few teachers who did receive a salary typically endorsed their paychecks back to the school.

Has something been gained in 40 years? Or something lost? Are things even all that different? Examine the "evidence," however much enhanced by time and repeated telling.

Bruce Gilfillan, professor of pediatrics, introduced himself at each first class with the jaw-dropping announcement, "I am the meanest son of a bitch in this room, and don't you forget it. I'm not here to be your friend."

Charlie Biggs, professor of neurosurgery, was also owner of a gun shop. He always carried a gun. In one class, he lectured for five minutes and then asked a question. After a moment, seeing no hand go up, he sneered, "I am so far above you," and exited the classroom.

Another time, after dropping numerous hints that he didn't think much of the new-fangled study aid of taping lectures on hand-held recorders, Biggs bought one of his own and dictated the next day's lecture into it. On arriving in class, he set his recorder on his desk, said, "Today, I thought I'd let my tape recorder talk to your tape recorders," pushed "play" and departed.

Biggs was actually a good sport. He was kidnapped one day on his walk up the alley to the back of the school and steered to the local watering hole, where the rest of the class was already assembled,

Ray Olson looks on as a student diagrams. Olson, a popular professor, suffered the fate of sharing a lecture hall equipped with signage that left him subject to pranks.

SEVEN TURNING POINTS FOR OSTEOPATHIC MEDICINE

Highly relevant to this day

By Russ
Gamber, DO, MPH

We know quite a lot about Andrew Taylor (A.T.) Still. He was born in 1828 in the very western tip of Virginia, the son of a physician and Methodist minister. His early studies of medicine came as a formal apprentice of his father. By the outbreak of war, he had remarried following the death in childbirth of his first wife, started a second family and settled in the Missouri Territory. So passionate was his disdain for slavery, he enlisted and served first as a cavalry sergeant then as an infantry officer, all with Kansas militia units. Despite his medical training, he did not serve as one of more than 13,000 surgeons in the US Army. He returned to his practice in 1865, supplementing his meager medical income with a meager income from farming in the lean postwar years on the frontier.

The United States Civil War stands as a time of rapid advancement for medicine. Indeed, all it could do was advance. As a Surgeon General of the Union Army claimed, the war was fought "at the end of the medical Middle Ages." Medical practice consisted of botanics — the study of medicinally useful plants — and heroics — bloodletting, purging, sweating, blistering and similar techniques. Almost 200 years after Antonie van Leeuwenhoek had shocked the Royal Society of London with his observations under the microscope, the germ theory of disease was still only one of many notions as to the cause of infections.

In 1864, the militia regiment Still had built up was ordered disbanded. He returned home to Baldwin, Kansas, to find that "the dark wing of spinal meningitis hovered over" his family. Despite all he and other doctors could do, three of the four children from his first marriage died of meningitis. Two weeks later, his infant child from his second marriage died of pneumonia. Still vowed to find a way to make medicine effective against such scourges.

As the germ theory gained ground among medical practitioners in the United States, Still remained skeptical of the value of using animal infections, such as cowpox, for vaccines for human illnesses such as smallpox. He proposed a natural vaccine using an irritant poultice on the skin to create an inflammatory reaction instead. His work had convinced him that where bones were properly aligned and nerve function and the flow of blood and lymph were not impeded, the body was perfectly capable of warding off infection on its own.

Museum of Osteopathic Medicine℠, Kirksville, MO [PH 971]

Osteopathy is a science which consists of such exact exhaustive and verifiable knowledge of the structure & functions of the human mechanism, anatomy, physiology & psychology including the chemistry and physics of its known elements as is made discernable certain organic laws & remedial resources within the body itself by which nature under scientific treatment peculiar to osteopathic practice apart from all ordinary methods of extraneous, artificial & medicinal stimulation & in harmonious accord with its own mechanical principles, molecular activities and metabolic processes may recover from displacements, derangements, disorganizations & consequent diseases and regain its normal equilibrium of form & function in health & strength.

~ A.T. Still's penciling of a rather tortured
one-sentence definition of osteopathic medicine

▲
The first graduating class of the American School of Osteopathy in 1893 after the first year of their two-year program, with A. T. Still pictured in the center next to the skeleton. ASO had begun the previous fall in a two-room house in Kirksville, Missouri. Within 10 years the school had grown to 300 students with building going on continually. As graduates left Kirksville, osteopathic colleges sprang up from Anaheim, California, to Philadelphia and Boston.

In June of 1874, all of Still's long thinking on the role of the physician came together in an epiphany. The key to healing lay not in fighting infectious agents but in restoring the body's God-given ability to do so. His techniques for restoring such functionality of the body he named osteopathy in 1885, from *osteon*, Greek for "bone," and *pathos*, "suffering." His manual techniques for diagnosing and treating derangements of the body came to be called osteopathic manipulative medicine (OMM).

As word of the effectiveness of OMM spread, a trickle of physicians began to appear in Kirksville. One of these was William Smith, MD, who became the first to receive a DO degree from Still. He was what Still was not. Where Still could discourse at length spontaneously on any joint of the body and the deformations it was

prey to, Smith was an organizer and administrator, and in the minds of many, the crucial sideman to Still in the founding of osteopathic medicine.

Rural Beginnings

By 1892, the trickle of curious physicians had turned into a stream of would-be osteopathic practitioners, and a two-room frame house on the outskirts of Kirksville was turned into the American School of Osteopathy (ASO). Building was nonstop, and soon an infirmary and a maternity hospital followed. Within 10 years, new schools of osteopathy had opened in Des Moines, Iowa; Chicago; Philadelphia; Kansas City, Missouri; Boston; and Anaheim, down with it. Communications and public health measures then in place were futile for such a disaster as the second wave. It spread and killed with response-defying swiftness. By the time the infection was noticed in a locale, people were sick and dying in mass numbers. It apparently killed by triggering an immune overreaction known as a cytokine storm, which is also apparently what made it so deadly among healthy young adults. Victims would often die within hours.

What was significant for the osteopathic profession during this disaster was that DOs reported far better outcomes than did MDs. Where MD drug-based care would average 12 influenza patients lost per 100 treated and 25 per 100 patients seen who had already progressed to pneumonia, osteopathic practitioners were losing only one percent of influenza patients and eight percent of those with pneumonia. *The Osteopathic Physician* quickly featured an article based on case summaries from 344 osteopathic practitioners explaining methods of effective manipulative care and crowing about the superior outcomes. The AOA offered reprints to physicians. This superior outcome became a lasting point of pride within the profession.

World War II

Though the Doctor Draft Laws referred only to MDs, there was no law explicitly barring DOs from service in the military as physicians. Indeed, both Congress and President Franklin Roosevelt attempted to enable it. Rather, it was policy set by the Surgeons

▲
Osteopathic physicians and older MDs held down the home front during World War II, and many Americans first became acquainted with osteopathic practice in those years. Here, a typhoid inoculation in rural Texas in 1943.

General of the Army and Navy, who dictated the terms of service in the respective medical corps, and DOs need not apply. The American Osteopathic Association lobbied strenuously in both world wars to have osteopathic physicians be able to serve as medical officers, but the efforts were decisively opposed by the American Medical Association. It was prejudice, yes, but with a widespread basis in state law and practice, too. And so it was that DOs of draft age who served did not serve as medical officers. Our own former President Ralph Willard resigned his commission in the Air Corps after his tour in the Korean War when he was unable to obtain a transfer to medical service. Many a wounded Marine or soldier was delighted to discover that the Corpsman treating him in the field was a fully-trained physician.

There was a stark arithmetic to a conflict requiring such a huge mobilization. The roughly five percent of the population that shipped overseas took 55,000 MD physicians away from the civilian population, which, at the time, was almost a third of the country's medical doctors. Osteopathic practitioners of comparable age had no reason to volunteer; they would be denied service in the medical corps. With doctor ranks rapidly depleting, the Selective Service System decided that DOs were a critical part of the civilian war effort, and those who had already established a practice were generally exempted from the draft. Students enrolled at osteopathic medical schools also were deferred from the draft, the same as for AMA schools.

The home front was manned by DOs, and hundreds of thousands of Americans made acquaintance with the osteopathic profession for the first time. Despite physician shortages at home, hospitals continued to deny privilege to osteopathic practitioners. As a consequence, the osteopathic community founded dozens of hospitals during and after the war, leading to notable improvement in undergraduate and graduate clinical education.

The Merger in California, 1962

Osteopathic medicine arrived in California with Aubrey C. Moore, who received his Diplomat in Osteopathy degree from Kirksville in 1895 and by the following year had established the Pacific Sanitarium and School of Osteopathy in Anaheim in association with a Dr Scheurer, an MD. By 1919, in the wake of the Flexner Report in 1910, the exodus of MD physicians to World War I and the closure of the MD school at the University of Southern California, the College of Osteopathic Physicians and Surgeons (COP&S) in Los Angeles (formerly the Pacific School in Anaheim) became the largest, almost the only, medical school in Southern California. DOs worked in the LA County General Hospital as attending physicians, and one-third of interns there were DOs.

The AMA Council on Medical Education dug in its heels. Using all the arm-twisting at their disposal, they arranged that DOs could not serve as interns — indeed, all association with DOs must cease — that the COP&S was no longer accredited by the composite state

Los Angeles County General Hospital became a battleground in the war between MDs and DOs. The result was a second public hospital strictly for DOs.

licensing board and that its DO graduates were no longer permitted to take state licensure exams.

The gauntlet thrown down, COP&S filed suit and prevailed. This led to a public initiative campaign, duly passed by the state's voters in 1922 as Proposition 20, to establish a separate osteopathic licensing board. With the American College of Surgeons as the accrediting body over all MD hospitals, including county hospitals, its demand was that DOs must practice in completely separate buildings with no association whatsoever with other MD medical staff. This led to a long period (1922–1989) during which osteopathic medicine would be officially segregated in California.

With the 1941 election of Forest Grunigen, DO, to head the California Osteopathic Association (COA), attempts were made to bury the hatchet, as his sole platform was to merge the DO and MD professions in California (the continuing inability of the AOA to gain the ability for DOs to serve in military medical service provided the greatest source of dissatisfaction). The ensuing discussion went so far as to propose statewide merger of the two professions in 1943. Both the AOA and the AMA stepped in to quash any notion of merger by the state-level associations. However, California's rapid post-war growth soon gave it clout at the national level. In 1951 Vincent Carroll, DO, of Laguna Hills, and John Cline, MD, from San Francisco, became presidents of their respective national organizations. Soon committees were formed within the AOA and AMA to explore merging at the national level.

At its Atlantic City meeting in 1955, the AMA House of Delegates was ready to vote to formally accept osteopathic practitioners and institutions and to drop its formal "cult" label for the osteopathic profession. However, members ended up accepting a minority report that required the AOA and its institutions to drop all reference in their publications to A. T. Still and to "osteopathic

concepts," going so far eventually as to request that "osteopathic" be replaced with the word "physical." This the AOA did beginning in 1958, though not giving up on the "osteopathic" name.

But California had other ideas. The CMA and COA were at the point of merger. The AMA gave its blessing, but the AOA insisted on maintaining "separate and distinct" status for the profession — over the objection of the California delegation. To stem the renegade tide, the AOA established the Osteopathic Physicians and Surgeons of California (OPSC) to oppose the merger. However, the bylaws of the COA arranged for by-district voting, which permitted the merger-favoring DO majority in each district to be counted as unanimous endorsement. Given that the 1922 proposition had been passed by ballot initiative, any change to the law allowing a separate osteopathic state licensing board would also have to be voted on by the public. In a campaign financially backed by the AMA, CMA and COA in 1962, California voted in favor of Proposition 22 to prevent the osteopathic licensing board from granting new DO licenses and to transfer its duties to the state medical licensing board when the number of licensed DOs became fewer than 40. State Sen. Stephen Teale, a DO at the time, wrote Proposition 22, along with 12 other state statutes enabling DOs to become MDs and practice under the jurisdiction of the medical licensing board.

Owing to the vigorous and persistent campaigning of Forest Grunigen, now converted to MD, who still wanted to see a national merging of the two professions, other states, including Texas, began to discuss the "California solution" as the future for relations between the two professions, much to the alarm of osteopathic practitioners in states with a more rooted concept of the profession. The situation in California even became a consideration in the rationale for founding our own Texas College of Osteopathic Medicine.

The California Osteopathic Association became the 41st Medical Society of the California Medical Association, and the College of Osteopathic Physicians and Surgeons became the California College of Medicine, an MD-granting institution, which soon relocated to the Irvine campus of the University of California system thanks to the efforts of state Sen. Stephen Teale, ex-DO, now MD. In 1968, the OPSC struck back, filing a suit known as *D'Amico et al.* against the state attorney general and the state licensing boards for civil rights infraction and trade restriction on behalf of several DOs who had newly moved to the state or who worked as medical officers on federal enclaves within the state but were denied licensure in California. At the same time, nationally, in 1969, the AMA changed its tune and decided to try to absorb the osteopathic profession and put it out of business by accepting DOs into its membership and encouraging MD residencies to accept DO graduates. As D'Amico prevailed in state court and the ruling was upheld before the California Supreme Court in 1974, California osteopathic licensure had to resume. More than 340 licenses were promptly granted to DOs arrived from out of state, the first since 1962. Steadily, osteopathic associations and institutions returned to California, the osteopathic profession nationwide found its legal identity secure and rapidly saw the last vestiges of state restrictions on its practice fall away.

Rapid expansion of the profession ensued nationally and internationally thereafter, making this one of the major turning points in osteopathic history. Eventually, desegregation of the osteopathic profession in all states and their institutions became reality, and osteopathic medicine was recognized as a separate yet equal medical profession that could freely integrate with the medical profession on all levels of education, training and practice. So, although the merger's intent was to obliterate osteopathic medicine via amalgamation within the larger state and national medical associations, its effect was just the opposite. It not only strengthened the osteopathic profession but was a catalyst to its unparalleled growth and development, making it the fastest-growing medical profession over the past 40 years.

Elmer Baum of Austin may have alerted Lyndon Johnson to end the service ban on DOs.

The Vietnam War

In the years following World War II and the Korean conflict, the American Medical Association fielded a steady stream of complaints from members departing military service that their patients had switched allegiance to an osteopathic physician in their town who had stayed home. President Dwight D. Eisenhower signed a bill, HR 483, on July 24, 1956, permitting DOs to serve as military officers on par with MDs. Public Law 604, passed earlier in 1946, had given the president the power to appoint DOs as Naval medical officers. Yet, the AMA continued to fight inclusion of DOs into the military — President Harry Truman declined to go against them during the Korean conflict — until 20 years later, when the California merger of the state osteopathic and medical professions made it impossible for the AMA to continue the pretense that DOs were not equivalent in training and education to MDs.

The story that floats around in DO circles in Texas is that this change of policy happened abruptly during a poker game when President Lyndon Johnson was visiting back in Austin. The late Elmer Baum, DO, was as well-connected as a man can be. He even loaned Steve Jobs and Steve Wozniak, friends of his son, $5000 to build the first Apple computer board. He was a wheel in Texas Democratic politics and had regularly played poker with Johnson for years. On this occasion, Baum pointed out that DOs were

Hailed as a Hero MD, Lt Cmdr Rich Jadick was in fact a DO. He did indeed save many lives during the Battle of Fallujah in 2006.

still not being allowed to serve as officers in the military medical corps, and Johnson, with his characteristic bluster, vowed to put an end to that nonsense right away. Whatever the case, on May 3, 1966, Secretary of Defense Robert McNamara announced the acceptance of DOs into military medical service on equal basis with MDs. On July 13, 1966, Harry J. Walter, DO, took the oath of office at Richards-Gebaur Air Force Base in Grand View, Missouri, stating, "As qualified physicians, members of my profession feel we should be permitted to serve, and as Americans we want to serve."

One might hesitate to make the case that osteopathic physicians are particularly well-suited to military service, but it certainly seems that way. In fact, DOs serve in our military at roughly twice the rate they represent in the general population. The first cadre of 113 osteopathic physicians to serve in Vietnam rapidly distinguished themselves through their medical skill and valor in the field, earning many commendations. The military branches care little to distinguish between MD and DO, and many an MD officer was astonished to find that the man he had just promoted or decorated was actually a DO.

The legacy of the Vietnam years for the osteopathic profession was that not only did the last major barrier to full integration of DOs into the medical world drop, but those DOs and MDs who served learned mutual respect for each other and brought that camaraderie back to the States with them, a spirit that continues to this day.

In one particularly vexing case of the blurring of MD and DO in the military, in the wake of the Battle of Fallujah in 2006, *Newsweek* offered a cover story, "He Saved 30 Lives in One Battle … Hero MD, The Amazing Story of the War's Most Fearless Doctor." Only, Lt. Cmdr. Rich Jadick was a DO, not an MD.

Managed Care and Medical Home

In 1973, in a move to curb the rapidly mounting costs of health care, President Richard Nixon introduced profit and competition into the medical world in what became a cluster of various techniques known as managed care. As the reform began to show promising results, there was wide adoption of managed-care practices throughout the nation. Within a few years, however, it became obvious that medical costs had resumed the same steep trajectory. Simultaneously, consumer backlash was forming.

Medical home is a concept promoted by the American Academy of Pediatrics beginning in 1967 to provide comprehensive patient care (acute, chronic and preventive) within an atmosphere congenial to patients and allowing physicians the satisfaction of focusing more on patient management, less on paper management. The concept was reinvigorated in 2002, when seven national family medicine organizations introduced the Future of Family Medicine project to "transform and renew the specialty of family medicine."

The concept behind both programs has continued to evolve and take on many forms in an effort to address the many market concerns. One tenet of both that has gone unquestioned, though, is the primacy of primary care. One of the major rising-cost factors was the former ability of patients to go direct to surgeons and other specialists. This resulted in some number of unnecessary procedures and hospitalizations.

Under managed care, in whatever form, patients must first see a primary care physician — family practitioner, pediatrician, internal medicine, obstetrician-gynecologist and, depending on the organization, some internal medicine subspecialties, such as geriatric medicine or allergists — for a referral to a specialist. There is little question this practice has produced major savings to patients, insurers and government programs. Medical home is less strict in this regard. As with HMOs, it provides more of a one-stop-shopping experience for patients so that they have only the one resource to think of in terms of their medical care. Still, as with managed care, it puts the primary care practices front and center, which plays to the strength of osteopathic medicine.

The benefit to osteopathic medicine is that, while we represent only seven percent of active licensed physicians, we represent one in 10 primary care providers nationwide, rising to more than 20 percent in several states. This has put our profession front and center in health care and caused the MD-specialist community to polish up relationships with us in order to be on the receiving end of our patient referrals.

Doctors of osteopathic medicine practicing today recognize the labors and sacrifices that have brought us to where we are now. I am particularly pleased to be able to shed this small light on a fraction of the effort.

- In 1960 there were six accredited osteopathic schools with just under 14,000 practicing physicians. Today, there are 25 osteopathic schools, some with campuses in multiple states, and more than 65,000 licensed practitioners. Already, 20 percent of medical school students are enrolled in osteopathic institutions. DOs are on the increase!

- All states now license DOs on an equal footing with MDs. Vermont in 1894 became the first state to accept osteopathic practitioners and California in 1901 the first to license them. Nebraska in 1989 was the last to license DOs.

- More than 2,200 osteopathic physicians now serve in the military, and UNTHSC's former president Lt. Gen. Ron Blanck, DO, served as Surgeon General of the Army from 1996 to 2000.

- An article in the *Journal of the American Osteopathic Association* discussed the finding that a large majority of MD school administrators had no objection to the core principles of osteopathic philosophy, with many embracing them as sound medicine.

With this great success, and there is no doubt it represents tremendous accomplishment over more than a century of hard work, comes fertile new ground for concern and discussion. With MDs now embracing many of our core tenets and with today's DO students too often seeing themselves as little different from those in MD programs, we are faced with the task of preserving our unique identity. For decades, when women, minorities and the not-well-to-do wanted to study medicine, it was to osteopathic schools they often turned. For decades, when poor or out-of-the-way communities received medical care, it was frequently from osteopathic practitioners. For decades, when people preferred a patient-oriented approach to the manage-the-symptoms approach, it was to osteopathic physicians they could turn. By working so hard to become equal, have we also become indistinguishable to many? Now is the time for our profession to embrace its heritage, re-burnish its values and keep itself in the forefront of health trends by communicating those distinctive values to the American public. ▪

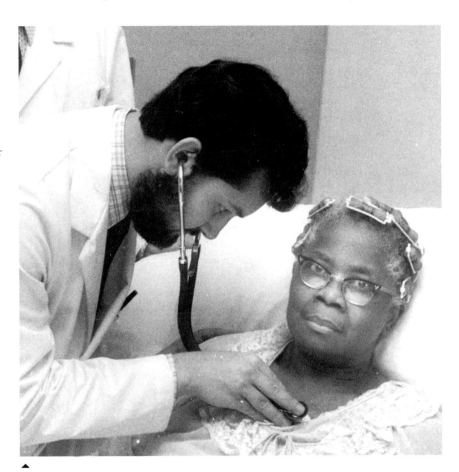

▲
Managed care and now the medical home concept have put a premium on primary care, a boon to osteopathic practice with its high proportion of primary care providers.

Andrew Taylor Still

Osteopathic medicine was born on June 22, 1874, in a reverie of insight in the mind of Andrew Taylor Still. He foresaw the future of medicine as naturalistic, holistic, drugless and based on man as a triune being, a unity of body, mind and spirit, possessing already "God's pharmacy" within as the means to heal himself.* Yes, medical science in Europe was beginning to correlate certain afflictions with certain "germs," but that was immaterial. Susceptibility to disease occurred when deformations of joints, muscles or nerves affected the flow of blood, lymph, "nerve force" or other resources to the organs of the body. If the problem was mechanical, the body's natural immunity could be restored mechanically, through knowledgeable manipulation of the joints and tissues.

For another hundred years, these circumstances of the creation of osteopathic manipulation provided a convenient excuse for some in the medical community to heap scorn on osteopathy as unsophisticated, a cult based on the ruminations of a single charismatic individual. To make matters worse in these same eyes, Still allowed in his autobiography that his creative thoughts had been much inspired by the success of his design for an improved butter churn (he was also a trained mechanical engineer credited with several innovations in farm equipment).

By now, a number of studies of scientific creativity have pointed to the flashes of insight that follow lengthy grappling with seemingly intractable problems. They are frequently aided by the synthesis of experience or know-how from other, completely separate avocations of the innovator. Was organic chemistry discredited because the structure of the benzene molecule came to August Kekulé in a dream of an ouroboros (a snake biting its own tail)? Was genetics tarnished because James Watson followed a hunch to create a possible model of DNA that turned out to be *the* model of DNA?

Still was born in Lee County, Virginia, on August 6, 1828, to Abram and Martha Moore Still. He was known as Drew as a child and to friends as an adult. Abram Still made his living as farmer and physician and served as a Methodist circuit preacher, a following that took the family to Tennessee and then Missouri. When his fierce anti-slavery sermons proved too provocative in those slave states, Abram was posted to the Wakarusa Shawnee Mission in Kansas.

As was common at the time, Andrew, by then a young husband and father, entered into a formal apprenticeship with his father to learn medicine. He helped with the administrative and religious

Andrew Taylor (A.T.) Still in a pensive moment.

duties of the mission, studied Shawnee healing practices, particularly bone setting, and mastered the Shawnee language. His admiration for the Shawnee was despite the fact that his maternal grandfather, James Moore, had been captured by the Shawnee warrior Black Wolf at age 18 and sold to a French trapper in Canada, able to return to Virginia only several years later. Black Wolf had returned two years later to the Moore homestead in Rockbridge County, Virginia, with a raiding party of 40 and killed or captured the many remaining members of the family.

Still fervently opposed slavery and was friend and ally to radical abolitionists John Brown and Jim Lane. Still, along with his brothers, joined in the many skirmishes from 1854 to 1858 known in the words of Horace Greely of the *New York Tribune* as "Bleeding Kansas." Even when making his physician calls in the countryside, Still had to be on guard for pro-slavery "bushwhackers." Once, he rode into a pro-slavery militia unit, some 50-strong, drilling in a clearing in the woods. Realizing his peril, Still blustered, "If you encounter Jim Lane in that shape, he will shake you up!" and offered to show them some better drills, which he did, taking over from the officer in charge.

Still was elected to the legislature of the Kansas Territory in 1857. It was also during these years that Still made his own extensive study of osteology by retrieving bones from Indian burial grounds, explored new approaches to the practice of medicine with friend and mentor Maj. James B. Abbott, including explorations in magnetic healing, and studied mechanics and machinery under Professor Sole.

Kansas statehood came in January of 1861. With the war following soon after, Still decided that

---

* "Drugless" was a distinct improvement in the 19th century when physicians' preferred concoctions still derived from the heroic school of medicine that were esteemed more for their dramatic effects than for any good they did the patient. Most were more toxic than tonic. When medical pharmacology began to make great strides during the next century, few osteopathic practitioners, most certainly not Still, held any reservations about staying abreast.

One fine summer evening, I was returning by the last bus, riding outside as usual, through the deserted streets of the city ... I fell into a reverie, and lo, the atoms were gamboling before my eyes.

~ August Kekulé, 1852

AMERICAN SCHOOL OF OSTEOPATHY.

▲

This four-story, 30,000-square-foot brick building replaced the original ASO frame structure in 1897, less than five years after its founding, to accommodate 15 faculty and more than 500 students. The new building contained the latest in medical equipment, including the second X-ray machine west of the Mississippi. Note tennis court in the foreground.

it was more important to serve as an agent in eliminating the scourge of slavery than in eliminating the scourge of disease. Contrary to many published sources, he did not serve as a Union surgeon but as a soldier and officer in the Kansas militia. He joined the Ninth Cavalry Volunteers as a sergeant. When that unit disbanded a year later, he formed his own company of infantry, Company D of the Eighteenth Kansas Militia, which he commanded as captain. He later advanced to major in command of the Twenty-First Kansas Militia.

When that unit disbanded in 1864, Still returned to Baldwin, Kansas, learning along the way that an outbreak of spinal meningitis was underway. At home, his worst dread was confirmed, and despite all that he and the doctors that he prevailed upon could do, two of his own children, son Abraham and daughter Susan, and an adopted child from his first marriage to Mary Margaret Vaughn (who had died two months after childbirth in 1859) soon died of the disease. Two weeks later, she was the only child of his second marriage, to Mary Elvira Turner. Marcia Ione, just turned one, also died from pneumonia. This left eldest daughter Marusha, 14 at the time, the sole surviving child. His helplessness in the face of this tragedy caused Still to vow to become "a Columbus" discovering new routes for the practice of medicine.

A large-scale Confederate raid demanded Still's return to service in the fall. He participated in the Battle of Westport (the "Gettysburg of the West"), receiving an inguinal hernia and a pair of minnie-ball holes in his

officer's greatcoat. Lean years followed the war for the family, which grew with four sons and a daughter born over the next 11 years. Still's hernia interfered with farming. Even a popular physician on the frontier after the war had a hard time making much income. There were only expenses connected with legislating. And the world was not beating a path to his door to purchase his innovative farm implements. Plus, as the Kansas militia had never formally become part of the US Army, he was denied a pension. Still did complete a course of study in Kansas City at the College of Physicians and Surgeons in 1870. Convinced that his ability to reduce dislocations and breaks in bones was unrivaled, he began to bill himself as the "Lightning Bone Setter." Business picked up.

Still's experimentations with osteopathy that followed his 1874 vision quickly convinced him of the soundness of his new approach, and he began to spread word of his successes ... disastrously. His own brother, Jim, claimed Still must have lost his mind. But that was nothing compared with the reception by his church, where it was received as the Devil's work and an attempt to emulate Jesus Christ. He was "read out" of the congregation. Perhaps their true motivation was otherwise, as Still lampooned years later in recalling the charges leveled against him.

> Lord, Lord, wilt Thou please stop him? Hast Thou not made opium, calomel, quinine, jallop, gamboge, blisters, and all these medicines for man? My, my, Lord, Thou knowest our very best paying members have large drug-stores, and Still will mash every dollar out of them if he is allowed to run wild ...

His ability to practice in Baldwin destroyed, Still moved to Macon, then to Kirksville, Missouri, population 6,000. In six months, he sent for his family to join him. He worked as an itinerant physician, away from his family for months at a time. By 1886, however, with word of the success of his methods having spread, he found he could stay in Kirksville and let patients come to him. And come they did, from all over the nation. Soon Kirksville sported two new hotels to house the many patients and interested physicians wanting to see Still.

In 1892, Still opened the American School of Osteopathy in a two-room house in town. The school flourished. Rail companies advertised their increased services to the 400 people a day seeking to come to Kirksville. In 1895, Still, a long-time believer in evidence-based medicine, began a study of drugs and approved a number of anesthetics, antiseptics and antidotes that proved effective. By 1902, the school had 300 students.

Andrew Taylor Still died December 12, 1917. There are now approximately 65,000 osteopathic physicians practicing in the United States. Jim Still, Andrew's doubting brother, became an early student and then enthusiastic practitioner of osteopathic healing. ▧

In the next day or so, Crick and I shall send a note to *Nature* proposing our structure as a possible model, at the same time emphasizing its provisional nature and the lack of proof in its favor.

~ James D. Watson in a letter to Max Delbrück, 1953

MAVERICKS IN A MAVERICK TOWN

Fort Worth's colorful history, osteopathic and otherwise

By Robert
DeLuca, DO

In cowboy parlance, a "maverick" is a calf that has been separated from and no longer has the guidance of its mother. The term denotes an independent operator, someone not particularly inclined to follow convention. Fort Worth's more cosmopolitan neighbors have long dubbed her a town of mavericks, and being a maverick town has long been a point of civic pride.

The maverick of most specific interest to us is Maude Russell, DO. She was instrumental in making Fort Worth the foremost city for osteopathic medicine in the state, which eventually led to the establishment of the Texas College of Osteopathic Medicine and eventually the UNTHSC. What branded Maude a maverick was an act that would seem not so unconventional today: she created a scandal in Commerce in northeast Texas by leaving her husband and putting her two young sons under the care of her sister to go off and study medicine in Kirksville, Missouri, at the school founded by A. T. Still.

She set up practice in Commerce, but in 1907 when her neighbor who provided her with buggy service went off to work on a ranch, Russell moved to Fort Worth and located downtown in the First National Bank Building. She was not the first physician in Fort Worth. That would be Jesse M. Standifer, a civilian contract doctor who visited the army garrison regularly from Johnston's Station (modern-day Arlington) from 1849 to 1853.

Carroll M. Peak, MD, became the first resident physician. He had attempted to settle in Dallas, then known as Three Forks, in 1854, only to be soon summoned to Fort Worth. Captain Julian Feild of Fort Worth was suffering a fever and dispatched a family member to Three Forks to fetch a doctor. Peak remained in Fort Worth. He and Feild became lifelong friends, and Feild's son, Julian T., would later study under Peak and, after completing his studies in Kentucky in 1869, became Fort Worth's third physician. William P. Burts, who had become the town's second physician in 1858, also became its first mayor in 1873.

The Base Hospital at Camp Bowie, a World War I Army camp on the western edge of Fort Worth. The Health Science Center sits on Camp Bowie Boulevard.

Hell's Half Acre was named when buffalo hunters and Indian traders were its patrons. It grew many-fold as cowboys, railmen, outlaws and Doughboys rolled through Fort Worth.

Fort Worth skyline circa 1920.

Downtown Fort Worth at the turn of the century, looking up Commerce Street to the Tarrant County Courthouse. The courthouse was built on the site of the original military outpost that guarded settlers against Comanche and Kiowa raids.

Dr Russell was not even the first osteopathic physician in town. That honor would go to Dr Thomas L. Ray, who set up practice in 1899. He was joined two years later by Dr Charlie Hook. Fort Worth Osteopathic Hospital would not be founded until 1946. A feature article in the *Fort Worth Star-Telegram* from October 30, 1949, as a new FWOH location neared its January opening, honored Ray for his continuing 50 years of service in the city.

Russell's sons, Roy and Phil, became osteopathic physicians, growing her practice and then succeeding her. Together they became physicians to the city's two most legendary mavericks: Amon G. Carter and Sid W. Richardson. These relationships became the backbone on which osteopathic medicine in Fort Worth flourished.

After seventh grade, Amon Carter left Bowie, Texas, unable to get along with his stepmother. He held menial jobs, most notably selling chicken sandwiches to train passengers, and slept in the back room of a barbershop. On his arriving in Fort Worth, his gift for sales landed him a job selling newspaper advertising. Soon he put all his money and powers of persuasion behind an effort to found the *Fort Worth Star,* which promptly failed to attract subscribers. Faced with disaster, he called on his powers of persuasion once more, attracting backers who in 1908 helped him buy out the town's leading paper, merging it to create the *Fort Worth Star-Telegram*. Within 15 years and for more than 20 years after that with Carter as publisher, the *Star-Telegram* had the highest circulation of any newspaper in the South.

With scores of friends in high places, such as Will Rogers and Franklin D. Roosevelt, Carter became the tireless public face of Fort Worth to the nation and the world. He also became a patient of Maude Russell. Carter's wife, Zetta, pleased with her own treatments,

was able to persuade her husband to see Russell. As Phil Russell later wrote, "Mr Carter ... was not well, given up for a cripple, a high-strung, nervous man, having lots of difficulty. His wife kept trying to get him to have my mother see him, and finally he said he'd never heard of a woman doctor that could do anything, but he'd try. My mother started to take care of him, and she got him over his affliction, got him up and out." In time, Carter became a patient of Roy and then Phil and a lifelong believer in osteopathic care.

By the time Phil Russell had set up practice in Fort Worth in 1920, oil prospector Sid Richardson had just become a millionaire. However, the up-and-down nature of the oil business soon left him poor again, and an oil-field accident had left him with a badly mangled and shortened leg. He sought osteopathic manipulative treatment from Phil Russell to relieve the pressure on his spine from the shortened leg. Russell noted in his memoirs that Richardson sometimes had difficulty paying for his regular care. They became close friends.

In 1933, when his latest oil venture succeeded, Richardson rapidly became one of the wealthiest men on the planet. Richardson invited Russell to become his personal and corporate physician. Russell declined. He explained to the affronted Richardson that he didn't want to take the risk that employment might damage their friendship. They remained close, and Russell was by his side when Richardson died. Because he had never married, Richardson left his estate to nephew and partner Perry Bass. Soon-to-be governor of Texas, John Connally, had also been a partner.

Carter became so supportive of the osteopathic profession and of Phil Russell, he resigned from the Methodist Hospital board when it refused to admit Dr Russell to its staff. Carter became, along with Russell, active in the planning, financing and development of Fort Worth Osteopathic Hospital (later known as the Osteopathic Medical Center of Texas) from before 1950 until after it moved to its permanent location off Camp Bowie Boulevard in 1956.

Amon G. Carter so supported Fort Worth that he was loath to spend a nickel while away.

Sid W. Richardson made Fort Worth home to the world's largest collection of western art.

Phil Russell took over care of Carter from his mother, Maude, and added Richardson.

photo: Courtesy of the genealogy, history and archives unit, Fort Worth Public Library

Maj. Arnold named Fort Worth for his beloved late commander Gen. William Worth, above.

Maj. Ripley Arnold, founder of Fort Worth, and his young bride Catherine.

"Longhair Jim" Courtright won fame for keeping the peace in Fort Worth.

John Peter Smith Hospital in 1940.

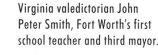

Virginia valedictorian John Peter Smith, Fort Worth's first school teacher and third mayor.

Richardson would provide funds for furnishing the new hospital. Later, Phil Russell would give final approval to using the top floor of Fort Worth "O" (as the hospital was known) for TCOM's incoming first class. The American Osteopathic Association and a pledge drive among state osteopathic physicians provided much of the school's startup funding. The Sid Richardson and Amon Carter foundations and the Bass family generously provided the balance needed for the launch of the medical college, and they have remained steadfast in their support over the years.

You wouldn't necessarily call TCOM's founders mavericks, but they certainly were out-of-the-ordinary visionaries. It was regular practice for George Luibel and his wife, Mary, to get together with Roy Fisher, Carl Everett and D.D. Beyer and their wives to socialize at Western Hills Hotel Coffee Shop. There they would dream that one day Texas would have an osteopathic medical school right here in Fort Worth. In 1965, Dr Luibel would chair the committee to investigate the establishment of an osteopathic medical school, and the rest is history that we have had the good fortune to live.

But the history of mavericks in Fort Worth long predates the arrival of osteopathic medicine and Maude Russell. For Fort Worth, the die may have been cast during its founding.

Fort Worth started out as a wall of green sapling trunks chinked with mud surrounding a parade ground and tent city, constructed by Company F of the Second Dragoons, as heavy cavalry was then known. The fort's founder/commander was Brevet Maj. Ripley Arnold, a hot-blooded, red-headed Mississippian.

Arnold holds other distinctions. He was, if not the most unruly cadet ever at West Point, then certainly a top candidate for the honor. He graduated, after numerous scrapes and close calls, with his class in 1838, a single demerit shy of the 200 that would have brought him automatic dismissal. He also stands to this day as the only member of the US military, officer or enlisted man, killed on purpose by a service physician (who was acquitted). Indeed, when he eloped with 14-year-old Catherine Bryant shortly after getting his commission, her physician father, a former Army surgeon, had vowed to track Arnold down and kill him, too.

After the Academy, Arnold posted to Florida to fight the Second Seminole War under Gen. William Worth. Arnold proved much more adept in the field than he had in the classroom and earned several commendations and battlefield promotions.

Numerous postings later, Arnold found himself in Texas executing Worth's plan to build a string of 10 permanent posts and temporary outposts strung across the Texas frontier from the Rio Grande to the Red River largely to curb hostile Comanche, Kiowa and Wichita activity. After overseeing construction of two other outposts, Arnold was ordered to erect an outpost on suitable ground near the confluence of the West and Clear forks of the Trinity River. After a spring deluge caused the river to spill its banks, the high ground on the bluff (where the courthouse sits today) looked more promising, and work transferred there. With Worth having died of cholera in San Antonio the previous month, in June 1849 Arnold christened the fort in the name of his beloved former commanding officer.

Settlers and merchants arrived. By 1853, as the frontier advanced and the fort was abandoned in favor of new ones farther west, the hamlet flourished and soon wrested the title of county seat from rival Birdville (which survives only as a school district adjacent to Fort Worth suburb Haltom City). By 1860, the population had crested well over 5,000. That wouldn't last long.

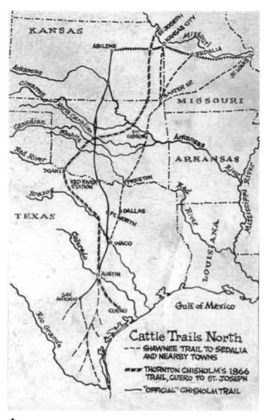

Cattle trails became the lifeblood of Texas in the 1870s following the tough Reconstruction years.

These days, many more tourists than Longhorns populate the Fort Worth Stockyards, a warren of gift and Western-wear shops, restaurants, watering holes and, of course, Billy Bob's, where buckaroos can dance to top country acts.

The war years and especially Reconstruction took a toll on Fort Worth, and the population withered to fewer than 200 before starting a climb back as the cattle business arrived along the Old Chisholm Trail. Fort Worth became known then, as now, as "Cowtown."

In 1875, the *Weekly Herald* of Dallas published a backhanded slap at its rival with a short report on the public meetings occasioned by the suspicion that a panther had been sleeping peacefully on a dirt street near the courthouse. The next year, when the Texas & Pacific Railway was completed into town, the stockyards boomed, and city promoters furnished up the little-remembered sobriquet of "Queen City of the Prairies." In a repudiation of the image of a declining, easily alarmed city, the citizenry informally adopted another nickname that had some sticking power, "Panther City." To this day, Fort Worth police badges feature a panther reclining at the top.

The Indian fighters and buffalo hunters gave way to the cowboys, and the town became home to a pocket of raucous saloons, gambling parlors and dance halls known as Hell's Half Acre. Such attractions and the rail lines brought plenty of out-of-town visitors, including outlaws. Fort Worth hosted, most famously, Butch Cassidy's train-robbing Wild Bunch for a short stretch. Stagecoach

and bank robber Sam Bass frequented the south end of town. The West's most famous con-man, Jefferson "Soapy" Smith, began his career in Fort Worth. Soon, Hell's real estate grew to cover more than five times its original modest confines.

The outlaws brought the lawmen, foremost of whom was Timothy Isaiah "Longhair Jim" Courtright. Known for arresting a good 30 men from Hell's Half Acre on a typically rowdy Saturday night, he enjoyed fame rivaling that of Wyatt Earp. A late career under the hire of cattle and railroad "robber barons," leading goon squads against homesteaders and union strikers and finally ending up on the short end of a shoot-out in 1888, left his reputation frayed even among his most loyal admirers.

Presiding over Fort Worth's rise from pioneer town to frontier rail and cattle center was another maverick, John Peter Smith. Smith graduated college in Virginia in 1853 top in his class and by the next year had set up Fort Worth's first school in the abandoned Army dispensary. When war came, he voted against secession but went on to become a colonel and war hero. Returning home, he acquired more than 1,000 acres of Tarrant County land and had his hand in a number of businesses. His gifts of his own land holdings were instrumental in bringing the railroad and other businesses to town, and in 1882 he began the first of his six terms

From the very founding, the desire was there for TCOM to one day become a full-fledged health science center with many schools. UNTHSC emerged as one of the few centers where clinical, research, public health and allied professions faculty and students share the same campus.

YESTERDAY

With state support, the emphasis shifted from the rigors of start-up to building solid operational foundations. A campus slowly took shape. New buildings rose designed to specific uses. TCOM became the cornerstone of a multi-school health science center.

Amid a changing health care landscape, the Health Science Center tried a number of new approaches. As several of these succeeded, the organization became increasingly confident of its purpose and its ability to innovate and meet its goals.

As TCOM matured beyond its lean start-up years and union with NTSU and resulting state support, more ambitious goals could be undertaken. Leadership ushered in a period of new vision statements, new partnerships, new research efforts and even new schools and programs.

I. M. Korr, PhD, led the effort to draft a new vision statement for the medical school.

Gib Lewis pushed SB 216 along with Sen. Betty Andujar.

but for no more than appraised value. While neighbors of the school were none too pleased to see that rider added, and some attempts were made at evoking public sympathy, in short order, Associate Dean Lemuel L. "Lash" LaRue was able to buy 22 properties, all at appraised value. The city also gave up a street in order to complete the desired 16-acre future campus — all part of today's campus — along Camp Bowie Boulevard, stretching from Fort Worth Osteopathic Hospital down the hill past the "bowling alley," the school's first home of its own.

The school pushed for a $71-million building plan. Medical Education Building 1 (now the EAD, for Education and Administration), slated to open in 1980, opened instead in August 1978, thanks to new prefab construction methods. It housed clinical sciences, administrative offices, classrooms, outpatient clinics and a library. Four years later, Med Ed 2 (now RES for Research) became home to Basic Sciences and Biomedical Research. Med Ed 3, opened in 1986, housed the Gibson D. Lewis Health Science Library, biomedical communications and a computer center. The campus that was created on the top of the hill in the Cultural District was a beauty, one destined to become all that much more appealing with a new development program presently underway.

Fourth, the school lacked stable

Dignitaries from NTSU assist Texas Gov. Dolph Briscoe (third from left) in breaking ground for the Med Ed 1 building in November 1976.

leadership. This was inevitable given the union with NTSU and the loss of the entire corps of the school's founding leadership. But North Texas State was changing, too. Legislation passed permitting TCOM and NTSU each to have its own president under a common chancellor. Willard was elevated from dean to president in May of 1981. When Nolen departed in 1979, NTSU found itself with an acting president followed by two short-lived chancellors in rapid succession. That changed when Alfred F. Hurley, PhD, was named chancellor in 1982. He would bring 20 years of steady leadership.

Willard had been assistant dean at Michigan State before arriving at TCOM. That school employed the health science center model of a medical school supported by research and by allied health programs, and Willard was an advocate of that model. In February 1980, with Willard as dean, a team headed by I. M. Korr, PhD, formulated, and the school adopted, a visionary statement of educational goals, "Design of the Curriculum in Relation to the Health Needs of the Nation." It was an effort to address shortcomings in health care by shifting emphasis more toward the promotion of health and wellness, less toward the treatment of established disease.

Willard had vision for the school and, having been a bomber pilot during World War II, he was tough-minded. When it came to protecting the interests of TCOM, its students and faculty, he could be counted on to prevail. He was an excellent administrator for large projects like the campus development plan. Trouble was, student board scores were dropping.

Alfred F. Hurley

Alfred F. Hurley, PhD, had a 30-year career in the US Air Force that began at the rank of private and culminated with two decades spent on the faculty of the Air Force Academy and the rank of brigadier general. When he retired in 1980, he joined North Texas State University as vice president for administrative affairs. Within a year and a half, he became the school's 12th president and second chancellor, serving for 20 years. His tenure was spent relentlessly upgrading both the reality and the image of what became the University of North Texas from a multi-county commuter school to a regional research university on the verge of becoming a national top-tier institution. The Texas College of Osteopathic Medicine was key to his vision of a major university system serving the whole of North Texas, and he worked closely with President David Richards to help TCOM achieve its goals.

By 1983, the number of TCOM students failing to pass the state licensure exams had become worrisome and was receiving unwanted notoriety in the local press. Lt. Gov. Hobby told Stockseth to fix the problem. Stockseth investigated and discovered that Willard, with fairly extensive backing of the faculty, believed that osteopathic legacies — sons and daughters and other relatives of osteopathic practitioners — deserved priority consideration in student admissions. The Texas boards, many felt, were slanted in favor of MDs, and the graduating students could take their DO degrees and go pass licensure exams in less-stringent states. Stockseth countered that those who did not show all signs of eventually being able to pass the Texas boards should not be admitted; the school's very funding was on the line. Willard resisted giving up any control over admissions policy, and in 1986 he was replaced as president by David M. Richards, DO. Eugene Zachary would begin his work as TCOM's new dean implementing the 39-point plan, worked out under Richards, to raise board scores.

Richards would guide TCOM until 1999. Indeed, it was not solely a medical school by the time he left. He helped bring the health science center model to fruition. The first research group, the North Texas Eye Research Institute, was founded by Thomas Yorio, PhD, in 1992. The following year, Yorio became founding dean of a new school on campus, the Graduate School of Biomedical Science, when the Texas Higher Education Coordinating Board authorized the transfer of the graduate school of biomedical science from UNT to the Fort Worth campus. Dean Zachary had worked out the details of the transfer for several years prior with counterparts on the UNT campus, primarily Vice President David Goldman.

On June 6, 1993, Gov. Ann Richards signed Senate Bill 346, and the combined schools, TCOM and GSBS, formally became the University of North Texas Health Science Center, or UNTHSC. All future allied schools would be brought in under this same title. And additional schools soon followed — the continuing culmination of a decade-old desire.

Despite the fact that this major change of identity was envisioned by and promoted by TCOM's osteopathic founders and subsequent osteopathic leadership, it was not without controversy in the state's osteopathic community, which feared dilution of the school's identity. Just the opposite, countered the administration: this step will greatly enhance TCOM's appeal and influence. The years have strongly borne out the validity of that claim.

In 1996, a new Bachelor's degree in Physician Assistant Studies won state approval. That same year the HSC and UNT collaborated to launch a new Master's of Public Health program, and the Cardiovascular Research Institute (CRI) was established, providing multidisciplinary programs in the prevention, diagnosis, treatment and rehabilitation of cardiovascular disease in people of all ages.

1996 was a special year, one of balls and galas. It marked the silver anniversary of the Texas College of Osteopathic Medicine and the golden anniversary of the Osteopathic Medical Center of Texas. Also, a grant from the Arnold P. Gold Foundation enabled the first

David M. Richards

David Richards worked his way up the ranks at the Texas College of Osteopathic Medicine. He became associate dean for academic affairs in 1981, vice president and dean for academic affairs in 1983, interim executive vice president in 1984 and president in 1986. He retired in December 1999 after 13 years as president and returned with his wife, Merilyn, to Ohio, where he served on the board of the Ohio University College of Osteopathic Medicine until November 2007.

He received his medical degree from Kirksville College of Osteopathic Medicine and by 1961 was practicing family medicine in Ohio. He became the founding chair of the Department of Family Medicine at OUCOM and associate dean for academic and clinical affairs before taking a position at TCOM and moving his family to Texas.

During his tenure, the transition was made to the Health Science Center. The Graduate School of Biomedical Sciences was added in 1993, the Physician Assistant Studies program in 1997 and the School of Public Health in 1999. Five "Institutes for Discovery" were established in aging and Alzheimer's disease, cancer, cardiovascular disease, vision and physical medicine, and the DNA/Identity Laboratory opened in 1990.

Medical Education Building 3 opened in 1986, with the four-story library it housed being dedicated as the Gibson D. Lewis Health Science Library in 1993. The six-story Patient Care Center also opened in 1997. TCOM's clinical practice plan grew into Tarrant County's largest multi-specialty group practice, a distinction maintained to this day. The entire campus went smoke-free in 1987 — the first medical school in the state to do so.

Richards was the first DO elected to the National Board of Medical Examiners and one of the first appointed to the Veteran's Administration Special Medical Advisory Group. He chaired the board of governors of the American Association of Colleges of Osteopathic Medicine. In Fort Worth, he chaired the Strategy 2000 Biomedical Technology Planning Committee, which led to the 1998 launch of the MedTech business incubator, a continuing partner in the HSC's biomedical research and development programs, now known as TECH Fort Worth.

TCOM's physiology faculty in 1981. Front row (l-r): James Caffrey, Carl Jones, Janet Parker and Patti Gwirtz. Rear: Verney Sallee, David Barker, John Gaugl, Richard Sinclair and Peter Raven.

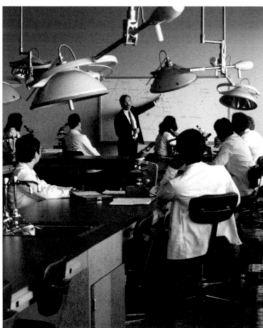

A pharmacology lecture in the interdisciplinary lab in Medical Education Building 1.

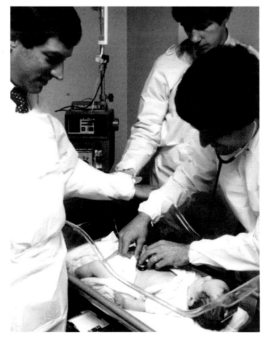

Class of 1975 graduate and faculty member Richard Hochberger, left, working with students and infant during the mid-1980s.

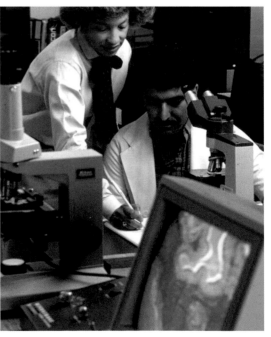

The advent of the personal computer in this era radically improved the laboratory environment.

within four years. With that sort of growth, recruiting is high on Vishwanatha's mind, "In the five years I've been at this institution, I've had no trouble recruiting top faculty. Fort Worth is definitely a draw. We could use more funding to pay them sometimes, but Fort Worth and the Health Science Center are real attractors."

Vishwanatha himself arrived from the University of Nebraska Medical Center, along with his wife, Lavi, and a son and daughter both now in medical school. He is a widely published researcher on the mechanisms for the progression of cancer.

Graduate education became associated with TCOM in 1972 when basic science classes for students started being offered at the North Texas State campus in Denton. Graduate students in the biological sciences shared classes with medical students, and TCOM and NTSU professors received dual appointments. This arrangement continued even after the TCOM basic sciences returned to Fort Worth; by 1992 more than 70 UNT graduate students in various biological disciplines were getting all their training in laboratories in courses taught by TCOM faculty. Because it was recognized that these students' career options would be enhanced if their degrees were in biomedical sciences and awarded by a health science center, UNT and TCOM requested and received Texas Higher Education Coordinating Board approval to transfer the UNT biomedical sciences program to TCOM to form the GSBS within a new health science center, and that is precisely what came about in 1993.

The GSBS leads all schools on campus, indeed, all health science centers in Texas, in student diversity, owing largely to student/faculty outreach being a driving concern of Founding Dean Thomas Yorio and furthered by Associate Dean Robert Kaman and the current Dean Jamboor Vishwanatha. ▄

▲
At the HSC, Thomas Yorio introduces students of the High School for the Medical Professions, a magnet program housed at Fort Worth's North Side High School, to medical research. TCOM sponsored the program beginning in 1984.

Thomas Yorio

Thomas Yorio has devoted his life to two pursuits: researching glaucoma and expanding the mission of the University of North Texas Health Science Center. After receiving a PhD in pharmacology from Mount Sinai School of Medicine and a postdoctoral stint there, Yorio headed for Denton, Texas, to join TCOM's basic science program as assistant professor. He rose in rank to become professor of Pharmacology and Neuroscience.

In 1992, he forged a groundbreaking research relationship with Alcon, a growing company located in Fort Worth that provides sterile ophthalmic products. The resulting North Texas Eye Research Institute continues to this day. The following year saw Yorio tabbed to serve as founding dean for the new Graduate School of Biomedical Sciences, a position he continued in for 14 years. In 2007, he became executive vice president of academic affairs and research, to which the position of provost was added in 2008.

His own research efforts in the area of glaucoma have yielded a number of important breakthroughs for understanding the disease's mechanisms and ways to treat it more effectively. Yorio has served in numerous national leadership and academic editorial roles in the fields of research, pharmacology and ophthalmology, and he has been enormously successful at obtaining funding for his own and other research conducted at GSBS. He also implemented a wide array of minority recruitment programs within the GSBS that earned the designation Role Model Institution from the NIH-sponsored Minority Access, Inc., and the 2001 NSF Presidential Award for Science Mentoring Outreach.

Yorio and his wife, Elena, reside in Fort Worth and nearby Burleson. Their two married children and three grandchildren also live in Texas.

"We have to create new knowledge as well as teach it. " — Robert Gracy, Biochemistry.

A research student presents her work to judges at the annual Research Appreciation Day.

Discoveries in UNTHSC labs have led to more than 30 patents to date.

Adeline and George McQueen Foundation UNTHSC Center for Research Management

Where is research carried out at the Health Science Center? All around the UNTHSC campus. Researchers from each of the four schools — the Texas College of Osteopathic Medicine, the Graduate School of Biomedical Sciences, the School of Public Health and the School of Health Professions — are busy researching biomedical topics likely to impact the health and well-being of Texans. The Health Institutes of Texas were established in 2007 to provide a way for researchers from all four schools to work together and move research findings from the bench to the bedside to the community.

How is all of this effort supported and coordinated? By the Adeline and George McQueen Foundation UNTHSC Center for Research Management, also known on campus as the Research Office. Glenn Dillon, PhD, vice president of research for the Health Science Center, oversees this office's seven divisions.

Much of the research is conducted in animal or human models. Egeenee Daniels, DVM, oversees animal-model aspects of UNTHSC research. The Office for the Protection of Human Subjects, under Brian Gladue, PhD, provides oversight to any project that uses people as subjects.

The Office of Research Compliance, under Rhonda Dash, MPH, insures that research adheres to all applicable laws and to the HSC's policies and helps researchers navigate the maze of regulations involving such concerns as bio-safety, conflicts of interest and research review boards. The Office of Grants and Contracts Management, led by LeAnn Forsberg, helps researchers submit their project ideas for funding and manage their funding once it is received.

Other Research Office divisions assist researchers to identify promising projects and move them all the way through to fruition. The Office of Strategic Research Initiatives, under Peggy Smith-Barbaro, PhD, identifies promising areas of investigation and prepares researchers to take on the challenges of innovative projects. Clinical Trials, under Michael Bergamini, PhD, helps HSC researchers conduct research for others, such as pharmaceutical companies preparing to bring new products to market. The Office of Technology Transfer & Commercialization, under Robert McClain, PhD, assists researchers to protect and commercialize products and methods they have discovered in the course of their research. This sometimes includes handing projects along to TECH Fort Worth, a closely associated business incubator that can help jump-start business formation.

The outcome of collaboration between the divisions of the UNTHSC Research Office and HSC researchers can be summed up in one sentence: UNTHSC currently has the highest rate of research growth of all Texas health science centers.

SCHOOL OF PUBLIC HEALTH

A lot of things that "didn't" are public health.

- The glass of water you drank that didn't give you intestinal parasites
- The smoke you didn't inhale the last time you enjoyed a restaurant meal
- The asthmatic who didn't need to use an emergency room thanks to an air quality warning
- The flu you didn't get because you did get a vaccination
- The asbestos you didn't breathe in from your ceiling tile because it is not there

Dean Fernando Treviño,
1996-2007

There is no easy way to define what in fact public health is because it is largely about keeping our lives free of harm, threats and irritants. Public health professionals work almost anywhere, from the highest offices of government to hospitals and universities to insurance firms and community clinics to oil platforms and manufacturing plants to playgrounds and remote villages.

They take on an unlimited range of tasks: change and advocate laws and policies; track and predict using statistical tools; weigh costs and benefits; research most-effective methods; raise community support; raise public awareness; raise standards of safety in the workplace; and marshal personnel and resources to where they can do the most good in the event of a disaster or disease outbreak. If doctors are the soldiers in the field treating disease and injury, public health professionals are the intelligence officers, working behind the scenes, trying to stay at least one step ahead of those two foes.

Public health professionals work with almost any definable group: meat packers, travelers and the travel industry, urban gangs, product designers, the rural poor, mental health workers, non-English speakers, the dating scene, cities at risk of natural disaster, facilities at risk of terrorist attack, truckers, manufacturers, miners, the uninsured and underinsured, polluters, handlers of pesticides and fertilizers, handlers of waste, handlers of

Dean Richard Kurz,
2007-present

Ximena Urrutia-Rojas works with children at Mitchell Boulevard Elementary School in Fort Worth to help improve their health and fitness.

bio-hazardous materials or carcinogens, disaster victims, toy and baby-product manufacturers, immigrant populations, nursing home residents, expectant mothers, new mothers, mothers of problem teens, drug abusers, drug handlers, drug manufacturers, users of multiple prescription drugs. You can begin to appreciate the never-ending challenge. It is most certainly a field in which it is not difficult to carve out your own niche.

Richard S. Kurz, PhD, dean of the School of Public Health, is bullish about the rapidly expanding

Eye-Opening Summers

My views have changed dramatically since returning to Fort Worth. The border is no longer some far-off obstacle that doesn't concern me or my safety in the Dallas–Fort Worth area. We are physically, economically and socially connected, and whatever affects Laredo has a good chance of impacting North Texas. In today's world, it is essential that we all not live in a bubble of ignorance.

~Matthew Lakich, MPH

Matt Lakich (class of 2010) penned his impressions as part of his essay "Reflections" after visiting *colonias* near Laredo, Texas, almost a three-hour drive south of San Antonio, as part of a class on border health issues taught by Terry Gratton, DrPH, and Claudia Coggin, PhD. These visits for master's students of the SPH have been held each year for more than a decade under the auspices of South Texas Environmental Education and Research (STEER), sponsored by the University of Texas Health Science Center at San Antonio.

There are more than 2,000 *colonias* with an average population approaching 200 people (more than 400,000 people total) in the floodplains along the Rio Grande that separates Texas and Mexico. The *colonias* are built along dirt roads in remote areas, shacks built of scavenged materials, lacking water, sewage and electricity, just baking under the South Texas sun.

Amid the appalling conditions, "students meet proud, hardworking people forging their version of the American dream in settings that might discourage weaker people," Coggin explains. This field trip is arranged to be educational. Students meet with various experts on border health problems — this time, rabies control and botanical traditional medicine. The students test the river water to find that it has too much fecal bacteria to drink, and they meet with families. The experience is meant as an eye-opener: Here, in the United States, exists a crying need beyond anything they ever imagined. Then the students return to Fort Worth and are assigned to write an essay entitled "Reflections." Once they have absorbed this experience, their work in the classroom takes on a whole new sense of purpose. With eyes open, their future trips into the field will be more about doing the work of public health.

Claudia Coggin with SPH students in the floodplain of the Rio Grande as they visit *colonias* near Laredo, Texas.

Inset: Working with Benjamin Cruz to extract invertebrates from a water sample to verify presence of *E. coli.*

opportunities opening up for graduates in public health. Kurz came to the SPH in 2007, replacing Founding Dean Fernando Treviño, having spent 29 years at the School of Public Health at St. Louis University, including eight as dean. "Keeping up with the public health needs of the world is both critical and non-stop demanding," he explains, "which is why we are continuously considering new programs and new ways to meet the demands of the field, identifying and addressing trends and preparing our students for the enormous range of challenges they will face."

The school offers master's programs in health administration (MHA) and public health (MPH) and a doctoral program in public health (DrPH). Beginning in the fall of 2011, the school is also planning to offer a Doctor of Philosophy in Public Health Sciences (PhD). The school's 305 students are arrayed among six departments: Biostatistics, Environmental and Occupational Health, Epidemiology, Health Management and Policy, Public Health Education and Social and Behavioral Sciences.

Many of the school's students are physicians or other medical professionals who wish to gain perspective on the administrative and policy side of health. The school offers dual-degree programs to students in TCOM and UNT Denton as well as to students at the School of Nursing at the University of Texas at Arlington.

In addition to conducting their own research, faculty in public health are sought after for the multidisciplinary teams of the Health Institutes of Texas. The faculty has grown from 28 in 2000 to 38 in 2010 with the expectation it will grow to 52 by 2015. ▶

Public Health is a field that can require slipping out of the high heels and into hip boots or sneakers on short notice.

Top right: Touring the State Capitol.

Center: Understanding water treatment.

Lower right: Testing the Rio Grande for fecal bacteria.

Below: Ann Blankenship teaches about nutrition and food ingredients.

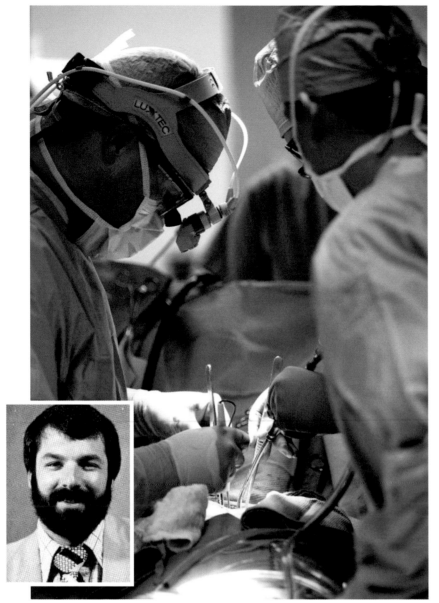

Jeffrey Alpern, class of 1979 (1978 *Speculum* photo inset), now practices cardiovascular surgery in Arizona.

Above: Orientation barbecues and other social get-togethers help student families get acquainted.

Below: Carla Butts gets hooded by Joel Alter at her 1978 graduation.

Bottom left: Medical school is a time of catching sleep when you can and where you can, including the Med Ed 1 Atrium.

Because it has always been tough — a challenge — there had to be ways to let off steam. Play, fun and time to get to know fellow students and their families could not be treated as intrusions on student time; they were a necessary and welcome part of the experience. This essential truth led to everything from softball league play (the TCOM jocks playing on the Nads were joined by the co-ed faculty/student Cadavers) to holiday parties, ping pong and potlucks, with a few talent shows and movie nights thrown in.

In addition to social activities, HSC students have always been proactive in forming groups around common interests. Often, these interests relate to particular areas of medical specialty, but others include spirituality, diversity, social networking and other themes. There was even a social fraternity for a while.

Activism has been another common thread through the years. "I'm not sure why," says Thomas

the class of 1978

Moorman, EdD, vice president of Student Affairs, "but the Health Science Center has always had one of the most activist student bodies in the state." Students can participate in the Medical Student Government Association as well as on a variety of committees with real clout. Some students choose to go beyond with involvement in the public affairs activities of local and national professional associations.

As the HSC has grown to include four schools, new spheres of student life have opened. For several years, students of all three types mingled in some of their basic science classes, but that went by the wayside as funding and class size grew. The programs may have "siloed" apart, but the campus itself had come together. Students closely shared the space, with the potential for more interaction. ▨

▲
The TCOM Boogie Band cuts loose on its 2003 reunion tour, with special guest Robert DeLuca, '84, as Elvis.

The TCOM Boogie Band

"Willard didn't like us, but Blanck was very enthusiastic when we cut our second album." So said Steve Bander (class of 1982), drummer for the TCOM Boogie Band. Bass player Daniel Saylak (class of 1983) added, "The Boogie Band was our alternative to sex and drugs so that we could hope to make it through medical school." Other band members were Mark Bander (free agent), lead guitar, David Fedro (1982), trombone, Ken Nowotny (1982), rhythm guitar, and Charles Suits (1983), vocals and guitar.

The band livened up student parties and a few other scenes during the early 1980s with songs about student life and medical issues of the day. "Virologist's Country Love Song" was their chart topper. As a parting shot for the school, they left their first recording to the Texas Osteopathic Medical Association to sell, with the proceeds to go to a TCOM scholarship fund. The band had earned more than a little notoriety in osteopathic circles (DOs in Florida sang their "Tort Reform Song" before a session of the legislature), and sales were brisk. But the band members were not prepared to learn 20 years later that the TCOM Boogie Band scholarship fund had $38,000 on account. The size of the balance was mind-boggling, especially with scholarships having been awarded.

Reunion Tour! That got the band back together in 2003 to cut a second album, again donating the proceeds to the TCOM scholarship fund. They heard sales were again robust, but they have no idea how much the fund has climbed.

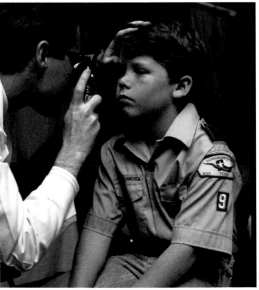

▲
Beyer Hall, first known as the Panoramic due to its broad curve and stepped platforms, was one of two innovative classrooms in RES. The second, Everett Hall, was originally called the Kiva for its intimate and informal Southwestern design.

Left: Third- and fourth-year students start their clinical rotations, one of which is pediatrics. Here a scout gets a checkup from a student.

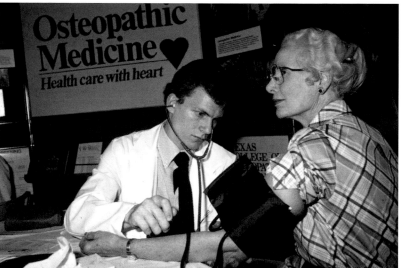

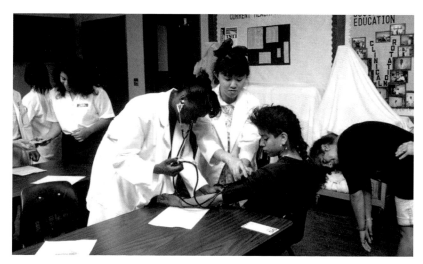

Dr Charlie Ogilvie

Danny Jensen

in the morning. He had become a compulsive runner in the prior three years as a result of efforts to combat depression during the life-threatening illness of his son. He had made the discovery (not without trial and tribulation) that running was the most effective and safest of the options he had been exploring.

Inquiring at TCOM, Weiss was told at the school that a chap by the name of Kaman was in charge of a facility on the west bank of the Trinity River down on University Drive. A door in the back of the Institute opened onto a trail that wandered nine miles along the west bank of the Trinity River as it wound itself around Fort Worth. They told him he would find it "near the Ol' South Pancake House." With that geographic hint, Weiss set out and found a large wood-framed two-story building that offered a total of 30,000 square feet. On the upper floor was the temporary home of the entire basic science component of the medical school. On the first floor was the Institute for Human Fitness. Weiss found Kaman and inquired about the Institute. Weiss listened as Kaman informed him of the details about the founding faculty team, their faith in fitness as a path to better health, the facilities and the mission of the program.

Kaman invited Weiss to his office, where he spread out ledgers and plans across his desk and began to explain the Institute's goals. Weiss, a lifelong native of Brooklyn, began to suspect he was being treated to more than just the famous Texas hospitality he had heard about.

Weiss explains, "I asked, 'Do you confide the business dealings of the Institute with all people who walk in?' He said not only, 'No,' but 'HELL NO!' Then he knitted his brows and looked at me quizzically. 'Aren't you the DO who is going to be our new medical director?' I answered, 'No, but tell me about the job.' "

President Ralph Willard insisted that a DO hold the position. Kaman found Weiss very much a kindred spirit. He told Weiss what to do if he wanted the job.

Weiss continues, "It took me about 30 seconds to say thank you and dash back to the school, where I practically barged into Dr Willard's office and begged him to release me from the contract I had just signed to join the Department of Family Practice so that I could assume the directorship of the Institute. He said that was 'fine with him' but I would need the blessing of Mr Jody Grant, who served as chairman of the board of the Institute while he was not distracted by his other interest as president of the Fort Worth National Bank. I was in Mr Grant's office an hour later and after an hour talking

running and fitness with him — he was a dedicated marathon runner — he called Dr Willard and told him he had found our medical director."

Early runnings of the Cowtown began in the Stockyards and wound through the campus.

TCOM President Ralph Willard with Cowtown winner Bill Parmalee and sponsor Jody Grant.

The race has grown, after more than 30 years, to include more than 20,000 runners.

Kaman and Weiss created a co-leadership for the Institute with Kaman heading up the exercise and fitness component while Weiss handled the medical aspects. Dr Ken Cooper of the Aerobics Center in Dallas assisted them in the creation of an Annual Health and Fitness Exam conducted at his center. It became the most comprehensive physical exam available in Fort Worth. It became widely popular, bringing in clients from all over the Metroplex, even the Fort Worth Police and Fire departments. It led to Speaker of the Texas House Gib Lewis and Speaker of the United States House Jim Wright becoming regular patients.

Danny Jensen, now vice president of governmental affairs, was then working for the Texas Osteopathic Medical Association and sent many members of the Legislature to the Institute. Their response was enthusiastic. Indeed, the Institute's two biggest constituencies were members of Fort Worth's political and business communities. Many members of these two groups would congregate each day at 5 in the morning and at noon for a five- or 10-mile run along the river led by Weiss or Kaman. It should be noted that many of these connections we forged became important in the further growth and development of the Health Science Center.

In a few years, the Institute reached a peak of 22 faculty members covering the spectrum of fitness and exercise health and medicine. Don Hagen was named director of Exercise Physiology, and Ann Blankenship was director of Nutritional Services. Medical specialists and PhDs covered most of the other needs of the athlete and the exerciser. The principles of fitness were emphasized and backed up with secondary research to make certain our message was sound. A paradigm shift was in the air; the public responded with enthusiasm to the concept of medical practitioners and scientific researchers available in a fitness center they could have access to participate in.

With the opening of the Med Ed 2 building on the main campus in 1982, the basic scientists exited the second floor above the Institute to occupy their new space. At the same time, the state was undergoing one of its periodic lean budgetary periods. The lease on the ideally situated facility was allowed to lapse. Without centralized facilities and access to a scenic running trail, the Institute closed in 1988. Now it exists only in the shared experience, which produced many valuable insights and forged a number of productive relationships, and in the effort that comes together each year to put on each annual running of the Cowtown Marathon. 🖼

◀
River Plaza campus

Where this building now stands, 20 intrepid students and a like number of faculty launched osteopathic education in the state of Texas with no assurance of success. 40 years, three new schools and more than 5,000 graduates later, their efforts paid off well.

TODAY

As the new millennium dawned, the Health Science Center turned from focusing on its own needs and directions to more active engagement locally, nationally and internationally. With increasing confidence, the organization seeks results in its core missions in a more strategic, disciplined fashion.

As this bold approach bears fruit, the Health Science Center is increasingly recognized for student performance and diversity, growth in research, social mission and community engagement. The organization has become committed to recognizing and delivering on the needs of Texas and beyond.

The Medical Education and Training Building, completed in 2010, is the first of 12 new buildings envisioned in the master plan to accommodate the Health Science Center's rapidly growing missions of medical education, research, patient care and community engagement.

THE HEALTH SCIENCE CENTER TODAY

Forty years young

By Jean Tips

Sporting a burgeoning student enrollment in all schools, the opening of a new state-of-the-art training building, unprecedented growth in research, patient care and community engagement — and a variety of national accolades to boot — the Health Science Center marks 40 years of innovation and leadership in the health sciences in 2010.

Collectively, we now offer nine graduate degree programs through four schools, with one potential school pending approval at this writing.

This anniversary prompts a pause to reflect proudly on the past and contemplate a promising future — one full of exciting opportunity but equally chock full of uncertainty. Serious decisions will be necessary to best serve our students and Texans of tomorrow as "the perfect storm" of physician shortages, health reform and financial recession will surely change the landscape in which we celebrate today.

UNTHSC in a New Millennium

Dean Marc Hahn, 2001-2008

The modern era arrived for the Health Science Center with the retirement of David M. Richards from the presidency and the hiring of Lt. Gen. (Ret.) Ron Blanck, DO, to fill the vacancy in 2000. The event that marked the transition most notably was the formation of the UNT System by combining governance of the Denton and Fort Worth campuses with the new Dallas Campus in 1999.

Dean Don N. Peska, 2009 - present

With maturation issues that beset the campus during the presidencies of Richards and Ralph Willard successfully resolved and the rigors of start-up under Dean Henry Hardt and President Marion Coy a distant memory, the stage was set for growth. Rapid growth on all fronts is

Former Surgeon General of the Army Ron Blanck is inaugurated as the institution's fourth president in 2001.

precisely what has marked the last decade and continues today.

In 2000, Physician's Assistant Studies was elevated to a master's degree program. The newly created School of Public Health collaborated with the city's Public Health Department to provide the community's first African-American Health Fair.

Blanck was inaugurated as the institution's fourth president in 2001, and Marc B. Hahn, DO, was named Dean of TCOM. The Osteopathic Research Center (ORC) was founded on the campus the same year with an initial $1.1-million grant from the American Osteopathic Foundation, American Osteopathic Association and American Association of Colleges of Osteopathic Medicine to foster nationwide collaborative research on the efficacy of osteopathic manipulative medicine. The success of the ORC is directly attributable to these entities and its long term, major funder, the Osteopathic Heritage Foundation. The Texas Missing Persons DNA Database was also established on campus with funding provided by the Texas State Attorney General's Crime Victims' Compensation Fund.

All campus clinics came under one roof when the remaining four floors of the Patient Care Center were completed. The East and West Parking Garages, including a rooftop garden and plaza, were

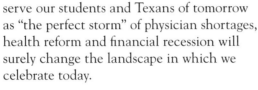

Ground is broken for the six-story Center for BioHealth in 2002.

The Center for BioHealth, shown at night, houses research and public health programs.

constructed, with the additional benefit of offering Cultural District visitors free public parking on nights and weekends.

Accolades were plentiful. The following year, TCOM was ranked for the first time among the Top 50 medical schools in the nation in primary care by *US News & World Report*. The Graduate School of Biomedical Sciences received the National Science Foundation's Presidential Award for Excellence in Science Mentoring.

Construction began on what would become the Center for BioHealth, a $40-million, six-story building for biotechnology research and public health programs, as well as additional classrooms, laboratories and a multi-dimensional imaging center.

By 2003, total campus enrollment exceeded 1,000 students. The Physician Assistant Studies program was strengthened with approval to grant Master of Physician Assistant Studies (MPAS) degrees, and for the first time, was nationally ranked — 33rd by *US News & World Report*. The ranking also listed the Geriatrics program 15th and the Texas College of Osteopathic Medicine 20th in primary care. The Texas Missing Persons DNA Database, housed in the campus DNA Identity Lab, made its first identification.

The Center for BioHealth opened, representing the first campus facility to be built with a combination of public and private funds. On the other hand, the Osteopathic Medical Center of Texas, formerly TCOM's main teaching hospital, closed its doors owing to financial difficulty. Alumni Plaza, the inviting tree-shaded green space above the West Parking Garage, was dedicated as a tribute to the more than 3,000 students who had graduated since the institution's founding.

In 2005, the university purchased the former OMCT property, adding 15 acres to the size of the Cultural District campus. In collaboration with Radiology

Associates of Tarrant County, the Health Science Center opened the state-of-the-art Center for Non-Invasive Imaging in the new Center for BioHealth facility, offering a wide range of diagnostic scanning services. UNTHSC also designated three labs in the Center for BioHealth for use by small start-up biotechnology companies working with TECH Fort Worth, a nonprofit business incubator.

The HSC strengthened its clinical education program with the Tarrant County Hospital District to provide expanded clinical and education services to John Peter Smith Hospital and the JPS Health Network.

The next year became a dramatic point for growth and cultural change for the HSC. In an historic move for the physician faculty practice plan, the University of North Texas Physicians Group added approximately 100 new clinical faculty members from the North Texas Affiliated Medical Group, creating UNT Health, the largest multi-specialty physician group in Tarrant County. This expansion, which doubled the size of the faculty practice, allowed the group to provide clinical services in obstetrics and gynecology, orthopedics, podiatry, psychiatry, cardiology, rheumatology, outpatient community medicine and oversight of the related graduate medical education programs at John Peter Smith Hospital.

UNTHSC entered the field of proteomics research with the installation of a $1-million, state-of-the-art mass spectrometer, the most powerful in the Metroplex.

Upon Blanck's retirement, Scott Ransom, DO, MBA, MPH, was selected as the institution's fifth president. One of his first acts was to organize the campus' 10 (now 12) research centers to form the Health Institutes of Texas with the goal of speeding clinical and scientific research results from the bench to the bedside.

UNTHealth
The Physician Group of the UNT Health Science Center

Ronald R. Blanck

Ron Blanck graduated from the Philadelphia College of Osteopathic Medicine and practiced internal medicine. As a surgeon in Vietnam in 1968, he began what would become an illustrious military career. He rose through the ranks, eventually commanding the Walter Reed Medical Center North Atlantic Region Medical Command and directing Medical Corps Affairs for the US Army Surgeon General. Blanck served as the US Army Surgeon General and Medical Command (MEDCOM) Commander from 1996 to 2000 with more than 46,000 active duty soldiers and 26,000 civilians in his command.

Blanck held teaching positions at the Uniformed Services University School of Medicine, Howard University School of Medicine, Georgetown University, George Washington University and the University of Texas Health Science Center at San Antonio. His 32-year military career culminated as Surgeon General of the US Army and commander of the US Army Medical Command.

He retired from service in 2000 as a lieutenant general and soon was selected to serve as president of the University of North Texas Health Science Center. He retired in 2006 and returned to the Washington, DC, area. His tenure was marked by rapid expansion on several fronts. The number of students doubled to 1,000. The six-story Center for BioHealth was constructed, as were several other critically needed facilities, such as parking garages. Under Blanck's leadership, the basic science departments were coalesced under the Graduate School of Biomedical Sciences, a move that resulted in greater collaborative research efforts among the basic science faculty and increased funding from the National Institutes of Health.

Equally significant was the growth in external relationships under Blanck. Partnerships with local hospitals increased; existing ones grew and new ones were forged. He partnered with the city to create TECH Fort Worth, a biotechnology incubator, to support commercializing the research discoveries being made on campus. He took an active role in bringing the first federally funded community health clinic to Fort Worth.

TCOM's first two endowed chairs were added: the Osteopathic Heritage Foundation Distinguished Chair in Clinical Research and the Dallas Southwest Osteopathic Physicians Chair in Clinical Geriatrics. Collaboration with Radiology Associates of Tarrant County brought a cutting-edge imaging center to the campus.

Blanck was also instrumental in forging new national-level relationships. He chaired task forces on bioterrorism for the Texas Medical Association and the American Osteopathic Association, also consulting as an authority on bioterrorism and medical response to mass casualty incidents resulting from weapons of mass destruction. Both the national Osteopathic Research Center and the Texas Missing Persons DNA Database were founded in 2001. The increased national visibility helped TCOM obtain its first Top 50 ranking for primary care among all medical schools from *US News & World Report,* and the Graduate School of Biomedical Sciences was honored with the National Science Foundation's Presidential Award for Excellence in Science Mentoring.

▲ From his inauguration gala to organizational holidays, three-star Gen. Ron Blanck was always ready to take on any role, from Heart Man to master of ceremonies.

Laszlo and Katalin Prokai use the most powerful mass spectrometer in North Texas for their research into aging neurodegenerative diseases and biodefenses.

Mayor Mike Moncrief (fourth from left) joins UNTHSC and TECH Fort Worth leaders, board members and clients in the 2009 Acceleration Lab ribbon cutting in the Center for BioHealth.

In 2007, the DNA Identity Lab, now called the UNT Center for Human Identification, one of only three authorized by the FBI for use in identifying human remains, made its 100th DNA match.

The Health Science Center created its fourth school, the School of Health Professions, from the existing departments of Education and Health Psychology and the Physician Assistant Studies program. Warren Anderson, EdD, was named founding dean in 2007.

The schools' leadership ranks expanded as Richard S. Kurz, PhD, was named dean of the School of Public Health, and Kathy Forbes, MD, was chosen president of UNT Health. J.K. Vishwanatha, PhD, was appointed dean of the Graduate School of Biomedical Sciences, stepping into the role Founding Dean Thomas Yorio vacated to become executive vice president for Academic Affairs and provost.

The year 2008 began with the 30th running of the Cowtown Marathon, marked by UNTHSC, the race's original founder, becoming the title sponsor. The TECH Fort Worth Acceleration Lab opened as a commercialization partnership with the HSC Office of Technology Transfer & Commercialization offices to provide laboratory and office space to help "incubate" TECH Fort Worth clients.

Clayton Holmes, PT, EdD, was selected chair of the new Physical Therapy program in the School of Health Professions. President Ransom created a board of visitors as a new strategic advisory group with diverse expertise from around the country. The university also took the first step in its new Master Plan for the West Campus with the demolition of the OMCT facility and construction of the new Medical Education and Training Building on its site.

2008 ended dramatically as the UNT System Chancellor, UNT System Board of Regents and UNTHSC President announced a study, led by a 38-member study group, to conduct a comprehensive evaluation considering all major issues related to adding a parallel MD-degree program at the Health Science Center. The study group, headed by Kenneth Barr, former Fort Worth mayor and city councilman, comprised representatives from the osteopathic and allopathic medical professions, area hospital leaders, foundations, current and retired faculty, UNT System Regents, UNTHSC administrators and community and business leaders.

In March 2009, the MD Study Group presented its report at a specially called open meeting with the UNT System Board of Regents on the UNTHSC campus. Before deciding whether to continue exploration of the issue, the board requested that an academic and business plan for the proposed MD-degree program be developed. Thus, an internationally recognized consulting firm was hired to work with a UNTHSC core team of key faculty and administrators to develop the plan. After extensive public communications and town hall meetings, the board of regents voted in November to proceed with its exploration to offer an MD degree, requiring the organization to meet specific planning, partnership and private funding, along with specific assurances protecting the permanent vitality and viability of TCOM and the other schools on campus.

In August 2010, the UNT System Board of Regents unanimously approved the creation of an MD-granting program as a fifth school on the campus of the UNT Health Science Center.

2010 also saw Rick Hill, DO (TCOM '78), and his wife, Cindy, make an estate gift totaling $2.1 million, the largest single gift ever, to UNTHSC.

U.S.News & WORLD REPORT
BEST MEDICAL SCHOOLS 2011

Scott B. Ransom

Scott Ransom arrived in Fort Worth along with his wife, Elizabeth, also a physician executive, and their three children to take over the helm of the University of North Texas Health Science Center in August of 2006. Charged by the UNT Board of Regents to be a transformational leader, Dr Ransom led the institution to rapid growth, financial stability and renewed vigor.

Ransom's experience spoke to his ability to lead the institution to new heights. Not only did he have an osteopathic medical degree from the University of Health Sciences in Kansas City, he had received a Master of Business Administration from the University of Michigan and a Master of Public Health degree from Harvard University. He completed his residency in obstetrics and gynecology at Oakwood Hospital affiliated with the University of Michigan. He had also completed the Program in Clinical Effectiveness at Harvard University and was a graduate of the US Marine Corps Officer Candidate School.

He was a fellow of many professional organizations, including the American College of Surgeons, American College of Obstetrics and Gynecology, American College of Physician Executives and American College of Healthcare Executives. He was a past president of the American College of Physician Executives and chair of the Certified Commission on Medical Management.

As part of a successful turnaround effort, Ransom served as senior vice president and chief quality officer at Detroit Medical Center, a \$1.8-billion, seven-hospital health provider system. Immediately before arriving at UNTHSC, he served on the faculty of the University of Michigan in Ann Arbor as the executive director of the Program for Healthcare Improvement and Leadership Development and a professor in obstetrics, gynecology and health management and policy.

Ransom is the author of eight books on quality, leadership, women's health and clinical improvement. His most recently published title, *The Healthcare Quality Book: Vision, Strategy and Tools,* provides a roadmap to improving health care in the United States. He also has published more than 140 articles and book chapters.

Ransom stressed quality improvement, accountability, strategic planning, professional management and establishing a mission-focused culture at UNTHSC. The result was a kick-start with steep increases realized in degree offerings, student enrollment, financial reserves, fundraising, campus development and construction, research grants, faculty growth and expansion and financial stability of the faculty practice enterprise, UNT Health. A strategic plan was developed and used to provide a rational management plan for the rapid growth. The plan has been implemented and is proceeding well, with annual updates as planned to accommodate new developments in the academic health care environment.

In addition to achieving significant growth and improvement on all fronts, Ransom is responsible for several accomplishments, including establishing the Health Institutes of Texas, TECH Fort Worth Acceleration Lab, Rural Osteopathic Medical Education program, several institutes and centers, and realizing national best on the COMLEX licensing exam test scores for four years running. Arguably most controversial under his guidance is the UNT System Regents' approval of the addition of a fifth school on campus, one that would confer an MD degree.

▲ Students treat President Ransom to an international welcome.

▲ Carl Everett congratulates President Ransom at inauguration.

▲ Chief chef for Employee Appreciation Day.

And this October, 2010, we celebrate 40 very productive years since the Texas College of Osteopathic Medicine first opened its doors in Fort Worth, Texas.

Today on Campus

In 2010, the campus is responding to the demands of a dramatically changing local and national health care environment with curriculum innovation, expansion of clinical training locations, increased scientific research, a focus on both the health of the community and the inequities of health and care among special groups, the training of other types of health professionals and more bidirectional external partnerships.

More than ever, the stage is set for achieving the organization's goal to gain Top 10 status, a goal necessitated by the presence of only a single other medical school in a large and rapidly growing region. In the report by the Southern Association of Colleges and Schools (SACS) Onsite Visit Team in Spring 2010, the Health Science Center not only achieves full accreditation for another 10 years, it receives praise for faculty dedication to student success and the organization's aggressive approach to quality. Forecasting that the Health Science Center could be a national model for other health science centers, they reported, "The institution's leadership team, with the support of the faculty and staff, has driven impressive institutional advancements in the university's areas of focus over recent years."

The Health Science Center Board of Visitors provides high-level strategic advice to Dr Ransom and the school leadership in semi-annual meetings, shown here in 2009.

Texas College of Osteopathic Medicine

Our founding school, the Texas College of Osteopathic Medicine, remains a strong cornerstone poised to fill a future that will critically need primary care physicians. It is unique among the state's nine medical schools as the sole source of an osteopathic medical education for aspiring physicians and surgeons in Texas. It excels nationally through its innovative curriculum, commitment to student success and outstanding student performance in the classroom, clinics and community.

Named for nine consecutive years as one of the nation's Top 50 medical schools for primary care training, TCOM now ranks third in the number of physicians trained in comprehensive primary care and rural medicine, 11th for family medicine, 15th in geriatrics and 22nd in rural medicine.

Approximately 65 percent of TCOM's graduates today practice primary care medicine (family practice, general internal medicine, obstetrics and gynecology, pediatrics and related specialties), with 54 percent of those remaining in Texas to practice, helping reduce the shortage of physicians in our state's communities. Many others successfully practice in more than 50 specialty areas ranging from aerospace medicine to vascular medicine.

For the fourth year in a row, *Hispanic Business* named TCOM one of the "Top 20 Schools for Hispanics." And, *GI Jobs* magazine deemed TCOM a "Military Friendly School" for the second time, an honor that places the school in the top 15 percent of all colleges, universities and trade schools nationwide.

Most recently, TCOM received the highest ranking of eight Texas medical schools named in "The Social Mission of Medical Education" list published in June 2010 by the *Annals of Internal Medicine*. The study evaluated the social mission of US medical

The UNT System Board of Regents, appointed by the governor, provides governance to all system components, including the Health Science Center. Photo from the August 2010 meeting.

education by accomplishments in number of primary care physicians, distribution of physicians to underserved areas and number of minority physicians in the workforce. The study tracked 60,043 doctors who graduated from US medical schools between 1999 and 2001. It traced the graduates' choices of medical specialties, as well as where they ended up going into practice.

Bursting at the seams, TCOM received much-needed, state-of-the-art facilities in May 2010 when the 112,000-square-foot Medical Education and Training Building opened on the West Campus. As the class size grows, so does the need for clinical and graduate education opportunities. Rotation sites outside Fort Worth now exist in hospitals in the Coastal Bend area of Texas for third- and fourth-year rotations, and plans are being made to open programs in the Tyler-Longview area.

Whether they are the only doctor serving a rural community or a specialist at a major medical center, TCOM graduates distinguish themselves as leaders, teachers and scholars. With some 3,370 alumni to date, recent alumni have excelled in some of the nation's most demanding residency training programs, some earning the position of chief resident.

Osteopathic graduate medical education partnerships now exist in 10 Texas universities and hospitals, as well as in osteopathic, allopathic and military programs throughout the United States. Residency lists of today's TCOM graduates contain familiar, prestigious names: Cleveland Clinic, Johns Hopkins, Mayo, Bethesda, NIH, John Peter Smith, Ochsner and many more.

Academic Excellence

TCOM students now consistently score at the top nationally among all osteopathic medical schools on all levels of their required COMLEX licensure examinations. How do they continue to achieve

▲
Diane Havalda, DO ('10), and her father, James Havalda, MD, surgeon in Taylor, Texas, are pictured downtown. Diane is a member of ROME's first graduating class.

that high performance? Less time in the classroom, more hands-on application and better acquisition of knowledge.

Faculty use a unique problem-focused, application-oriented curriculum based upon principles and methods that include adherence to educational psychologist Benjamin Bloom's taxonomy of learning. Bloom's key insight was that knowledge-based competencies develop in a logical, progressive manner, and it is the latter stages of being able to work with information that characterize the deep knowledge of expertise.

Restructuring knowledge to make it more accessible and useful occurs with comprehension and application of information. The approach taken is that information should be acquired outside of the classroom by self-study of assigned readings, and that the classroom should be reserved for comprehension and application sessions. The faculty are taught how to teach this innovative curriculum through an "Academy" with dedicated training to support excellence.

An example of this model in action is the Rural Osteopathic Medical Education (ROME) program, led from the beginning by John Bowling, DO, which graduated its first 11 students in 2010. The program is for students who have the mindset, skills and willingness to practice medicine outside the urban grid. From the first year, these students are exposed to the rural lifestyle by living and working in small towns and underserved areas. ROME students see patients in-clinic, make hospital rounds, make nursing home visits and spend time volunteering in the community — the daily experience of a rural physician. Some 29 percent of all TCOM graduates practice in small Texas towns.

▲
Don N. Peska leads what continues to be the top osteopathic medical school in the nation.

Commitment to student success

What happens if all isn't going so smoothly for the student doctor?

TCOM employs a unique, proactive counseling approach, allowing faculty members and administrators to monitor each student's progress closely throughout their medical school training. It employs comprehensive academic electronic tracking of students, focusing on reports that are available on each student in real time. As soon as student exams are graded, the information is available online and integrated into the complete academic record.

Data are also available from pre-admission through the most recent test grade so that administrators can review trends and offer rapid intervention to students who are in need of career advice or academic assistance. Recipients of test scores below 70, for example, are immediately seen by a counselor. Scores of confidential services, from grief counseling to pet sitting, are available to help get students back on track.

Graduate School of Biomedical Sciences

At the Graduate School of Biomedical Sciences, students today earn PhD and MS degrees while working side-by-side with world-renowned faculty researchers to solve some of today's most important health problems.

▲
The School of Public Health under Richard Kurz seeks to keep whole populations healthy.

▲
All TCOM students get their basic sciences from GSBS faculty led by J. K. Vishwanatha.

The Graduate School is home to state-of-the-art research facilities and one of the most diverse student bodies in Texas. Degrees are offered in a variety of fields, and dual degrees are available through collaborations with other Health Science Center programs and schools. Graduates are recruited by the top research laboratories in the nation, both in academia and industry, for postdoctoral fellowships or employment. Of particular note is the school's MS in Medical Science program, which prepares post-baccalaureate students for medical or dental school entry. Almost 70 percent of graduates in 2009 and 2010 matriculated on to medical school — three-fifths of those to TCOM.

School of Public Health

The School of Public Health — today one of only 44 in the United States accredited by the Council on Education for Public Health — leads the nation in student diversity. Founded as a grass-roots effort of Fort Worth's community leaders and public health officials, its innovative research and nationally-recognized educational programs prepare students to address the health needs of diverse communities here in Texas and around the world.

The school has grown rapidly in student enrollment and research funding while maintaining strong and vital links with public health professionals in the community. Students learn to recognize the social, economic and environmental factors that affect the health of the public and gain the knowledge to take leading roles in developing policies that encourage and foster healthy communities. In 2007, SPH was re-accredited for the maximum term of seven years.

Physician Assistant Chair "Hammerin'" Hank Lemke.

Physical Therapy Chair Clayton Holmes

Research

The "new age" of the Health Science Center has brought a new appreciation for research as a prerequisite for a national reputation, a must-have experience for student learning, a critical source of funding for the organization and a catalyst for new internal and external partnerships. Areas of faculty inter-professional research strength include primary care and prevention, aging and Alzheimer's disease and investigative genetics. These and other researchers on campus currently help the Health Science Center lead all its Texas health science center peers in research growth. In the past five years, extramural research awards for our faculty have increased by more than 100 percent, a real feat given the increasing competitiveness of research funding.

In step with the National Institutes of Health "road map" directive to increase inter-professional research, Health Science Center faculty and students blend the disciplines of basic science, primary care and clinical and public-health research to improve the quality of life for all as part of the Health Institutes of Texas.

Our research influence extends throughout the world, with partner universities in the Philippines, Australia, Thailand, Russia, India, Scotland and Spain. HSC faculty members currently conduct research in Canada, Colombia, Hungary, Mexico and Peru.

School of Health Professions

No health enterprise in the last decade fails to understand the need for well-trained non-physician health professionals. These providers have become key to the team approach of patient care. The campus' newest school, the School of Health Professions, houses the Physician Assistant Studies program, as well as the new Physical Therapy program, to meet the growing demand.

In 1997, when the first students matriculated into the Physician Assistant Studies program, it was a department of TCOM. Then in 2008, the program was housed and expanded in the School of Health Professions.

Physician Assistant Studies currently offers a three-year master's degree program, the Master of Physician Assistant Studies (MPAS) degree. In 2009, it was ranked 34th in the nation by *US News & World Report* and has ranked among the magazine's Top 50 PA programs since 2003. Its graduates are highly sought-after providers. The MPAS program is accredited by the Accreditation Review Commission on Education for Physician Assistants.

The school's new Physical Therapy program launched in 2010 to offer the Doctor of Physical Therapy (DPT) degree. Physical therapy faculty will team up with physicians and specialists to offer unparalleled training in musculoskeletal and orthopedic practices, and osteopathic manipulative therapy techniques. The Physical Therapy program is accredited by the Commission on Accreditation in Physical Therapy Education and the Texas Higher Education Coordinating Board.

The HSC research effort led by Glenn Dillon is the fastest-growing in the state of Texas.

UNT Health

Kathleen Forbes, MD, leads UNT Health, a $85-million clinical enterprise, Tarrant County's largest multi-specialty group practice.

Growth of the academic side of the house has been equally matched by growth in the organization's patient care delivery mission. In 2010, UNT Health had more than 600,000 patient visits, delivered 7,000 babies and had 40 clinics throughout Tarrant County. Some of these are collaborative clinics with JPS Health Network, as UNT Health provides physician coverage for the JPS Community Health Centers.

In addition to primary care, UNT Health offers some 27 medical specialties. This year 43 practitioners have been named either "Super Doctors" by *Texas Monthly* magazine, or "Top Docs" by *Fort Worth, Texas* magazine.

Culture of Excellence

Today at the Health Science Center, "quality" and "excellence" are more than just guiding terms. Implementing the management systems that will reliably deliver them has required a change in institutional culture. It hangs primarily on two key considerations: stating desired outcomes accompanied by measurable metrics that indicate success, and holding people accountable for achieving those outcomes.

"Thinking Councils" have been formed in each strategic area of the organization consisting of top managers plus representatives from all levels working to develop and achieve the targeted goals and initiatives of organization-wide yearly and five-year strategic plans.

Thomas Fairchild, PhD, vice president of the Office of Strategy and Measurement, points out the benefit of this approach, "We don't just consume our own revenues like a for-profit company. We consume public trust — funds from taxpayers and from donors who believe in our mission. All the more reason, then, for us to perform at our peak."

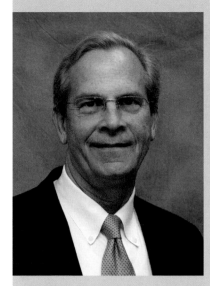

Lee Jackson
and the University of North Texas System

As the only public university system located in and primarily serving the North Texas region, the University of North Texas System has nearly 40,000 students and annually graduates more than 8,000 students.

The System includes UNT, the flagship and one of the state's largest and most comprehensive universities; the UNT Health Science Center at Fort Worth, the state's only osteopathic medical school; UNT Dallas, the city of Dallas' first public university; and UNT Dallas College of Law, which will become the region's first public law school when it opens in fall 2012.

UNT was founded as a teacher training college in 1890. Now the state's fourth-largest university, UNT is an emerging research university with more than 36,000 students and nearly 250 degree programs within 12 colleges and schools.

The Health Science Center grew out of the Texas College of Osteopathic Medicine, which opened in 1970. The TCOM is one of only 28 colleges of osteopathic medicine in the nation and has been continually ranked as one of the top 50 medical schools nationally for primary care.

Founded in 2000 as the UNT Dallas Campus, UNT Dallas quickly filled a pent-up demand for affordable higher education in southern Dallas and became a stand-alone university in fall 2010.

The UNT System's member institutions boost regional economic activity by nearly $2 billion annually. They are committed to closing educational gaps, providing high-quality education, advancing knowledge and supporting the economic and social welfare of the region and state.

A 10-member Board of Regents, appointed by the governor of Texas, provides oversight of the UNT System as provided by state law.

Chancellor Lee Jackson reports to the board of regents and has directed the UNT System since September 2002. During his tenure, he has helped expand the system's scope, visibility and impact on Texas higher education. Jackson played a pivotal role in establishing the UNT System Center at Dallas, UNT Dallas and the UNT Dallas College of Law. Before becoming chancellor, he spent 30 years in government. He began his career in the Dallas City Manager's Office, served five terms in the Texas House of Representatives and was elected four times as Dallas County Judge.

PRESCRIPTION FOR TOMORROW

Tomorrow's health care professionals in training today

In May 2010, at the Health Science Center's 37th annual commencement at Daniel Meyer Coliseum on the Texas Christian University campus, more than 400 graduates received their degrees in the largest graduation ceremony of the institution's history. This total included 152 new doctors of osteopathic medicine leaving the Texas College of Osteopathic Medicine for residency training. Also, 34 new physician assistants departed the School of Health Professions headed for clinical positions. A total of 132 biomedical researchers graduated from the Graduate School of Biomedical Sciences, headed for destinations such as medical school, research assistantships or industry. The 85 School of Public Health graduates moved on to positions in government, hospitals, academia and elsewhere. Several graduates received more than one degree. To this point in history, the students of all schools have graduated in a single ceremony.

In fact, the most recent era of the Health Science Center has brought a purposeful effort to remove barriers between the various schools, the better to prepare students for careers that will be enhanced by the ability to interact with health professionals in all fields. At the very outset of this era, the Office of Student Affairs, under Thomas Moorman, EdD, became centralized, creating more opportunities for students to interact — socially, academically and ceremonially. Previously, each school hosted its own student office.

Even the HSC's new Master Plan takes into account ways to further student (and faculty) interaction among the programs, and plans are underway for future students to participate in multi-disciplinary projects as part of the curriculum.

If commencement is the capstone ceremony, the welcoming ritual for some entering students is the White Coat Ceremony. New students entering TCOM and the PA program receive the white coat indicative of a student doctor or PA. This observance began in 1996 for all new schools' students as a way to welcome them to their profession while conveying a sense of the dignity and professionalism of the roles they are taking on. During the ceremony, incoming students take an oath acknowledging their responsibilities and willingness to assume the obligations of their new professions.

Other traditional annual events include the poignant memorial service TCOM students conduct in honor of participants in the Willed Body Program.

Fun is an historic tradition. Fall "Ranchland" and the DO Dash, December "Casino Night" and Spring "Field Day" are ongoing activities. Powder puff football games, played by two teams of the women students of TCOM cheered on by their male counterparts, are enjoyed by all.

The closing of the Osteopathic Medical Center of Texas in 2004 was briefly disruptive to student life, scattering rotations as far away as Corpus Christi. These rotations today involve a wider number of clinics and hospitals — a logistical curse but a gain in exposure to a much wider variety of medical settings.

The student body as a whole retains its reputation

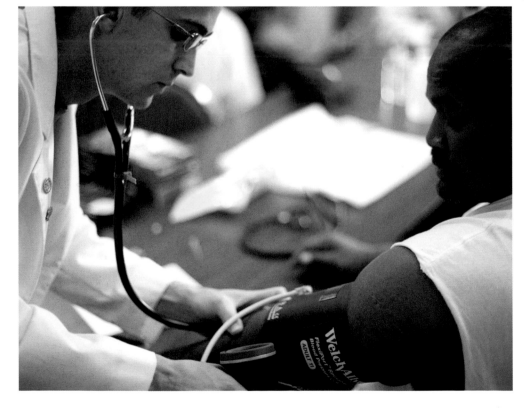

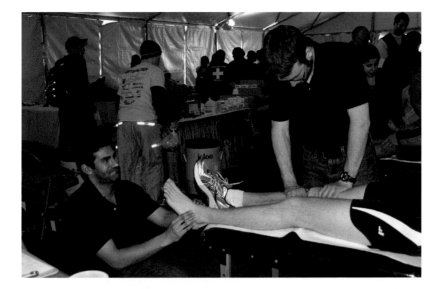

for political and social activism. TCOM students, for example, have over recent years started a clinic for Fort Worth homeless residents, brought care to other lands as part of medical mission trips and tended the victims of natural disasters such as Hurricane Katrina. In fact, the TCOM classes of 2012 and 2013 logged more than 4,700 hours of clinical community service during the Spring 2010 semester.

At the same time, the face of the student population has changed. In the 2000s, students are younger (the great majority coming straight from college) and more diverse, with female students exceeding males in number.

Students in recent years have reaped a comparable windfall when it comes to quality of facilities, educational methods, support services and technology — things quite unimaginable to those early students who had to carry furniture and armloads of library books up five flights of stairs in the "O" or who spent weekends painting a bowling alley to get it ready to hold classes. The student experiences of 1970 and '71 barely resemble what today's students enjoy 40 years later. Yet, regardless of the era, the mission has remained to train top-quality medical professionals for service to the people of Texas and beyond. ▓

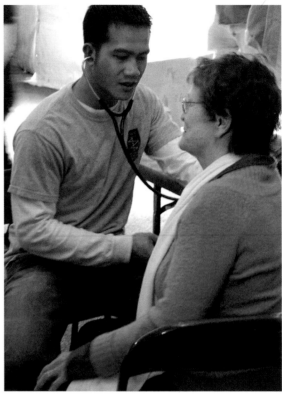

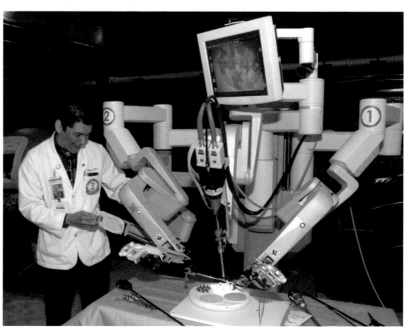

DIVERSITY BUILT IN

Ralph Willard, DO, was dean of TCOM from 1975 to 1985 as well as acting vice president and president during those years. These were years when the student body began to diversify. Diversity, he felt, was inherent in the osteopathic philosophy. "We believe that communities should be served by osteopathic medicine. It makes sense that African-American and Mexican-American communities would be most often served by African-American and Mexican-American DOs. As for women, A. T. Still himself said that, all in all, women physicians should prove superior to men in tending to patients."

The first TCOM class, the class of 1974, was conspicuous for the presence of but a single female among its 20 initial students — Nelda Cunniff. Cunniff was a nurse who decided to take advantage of a medical school opening not too far from her home to become a physician. With a long-time practice in Burleson, just south of Fort Worth, she shrugs off her singularity as being anything more than a product of the times. "If you look at photographs from osteopathic colleges before World War II, there are plenty of women. If you look now, it's more than half women. Those years were just different when it came to women's ideas about work and family."

So, what programs were implemented to begin achieving the diversity TCOM now enjoys? "No programs," says Willard. "We simply put the word out to DOs around the state to be on the lookout for promising young talent of all races and to refer them to us. That seemed to do the job."

To an extent, Willard's sanguinity about the ability of the osteopathic community to nudge promising minority and other candidates forward holds true for TCOM to this day. It is certainly the case that prospective students with a ready answer to the question "Why do you want to attend an *osteopathic* medical school?" help their own cause during faculty interviews.

However, TCOM's Office of Admissions and Outreach under Assistant Dean Joel Daboub, MBA, operates much more proactively than in the school's early years. All pre-med students become familiar with the unforgiving math of student selection: One in three applicants are invited to interview; one in three or four of those become part of the next entering class. The most recent years at TCOM have seen more than 2,000 applicants, yielding classes of just less than 200.

While the class make-up reflects the Texas population when it comes to numbers of Caucasians and women (with the 2010 entering class, the percentage of female students edges up to almost 60), the numbers of African-American and Mexican-American students remain below desired levels. The medical school sponsors programs to address that shortfall, including hosting high school science classes on campus to generate early interest in pursuing a medical career.

GSBS Outreach Director Robert Kaman with soldier-scientist US Army Maj. Robert Carter, III. Carter, an alumnus of both the GSBS and SPH, was also a graduate of the Bridges to the Doctorate Program to increase the number of underrepresented minority biomedical scientists.

Student recruiting efforts target colleges with majority ratios of black or Hispanic students and also participate, along with the state's eight MD-granting schools, in JAMP, the Joint Admissions Medical Program. JAMP was inaugurated by the state Legislature to provide a variety of supports to students from economically disadvantaged backgrounds attending four-year undergraduate schools in the state and wishing to enter medical training.

The Graduate School of Biomedical Sciences, under founding Dean Thomas Yorio, PhD, was determined to be even more proactive in addressing diversity. The school now has five outreach programs to work with primary or secondary schools in the Fort Worth area to identify promising minority students and alert them to opportunities for study and careers in basic science and research. Three more programs allow minority undergraduate students in area colleges to spend part of their summers trying their hands at scientific research.

Associate Dean Robert Kaman, JD, PhD, director of outreach for the GSBS, points out, "These are some of the most popular programs for faculty participation because of the opportunity to train young scientists and clinicians while they are still undergraduates or high school students. The students ultimately choose careers in medicine and the biomedical sciences, and after their experiences here at the Health Science Center, they return for graduate training. Several have gone on to become faculty members here and continue the legacy for those following in their footsteps."

The School of Public Health has the most diverse student population in the country compared with all other accredited programs.

With the addition of outreach programs for graduate students and for its own faculty development, the GSBS has earned national recognition, including being designated a Role Model Institution by Minority Access, Inc., sponsored by the National Institutes of Health and being awarded the National Science Foundation Presidential Award for Science Mentoring Outreach by President Bill Clinton. The school has achieved the most diverse student body of any health science center in the state.

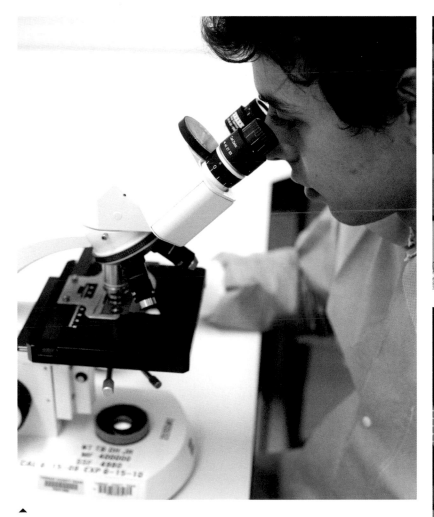

Students and teachers of all levels — elementary through undergraduate — participate in summer outreach programs on campus, many of them focused on providing minority groups an introduction to science and medicine as potential career paths.

WORKING WITH AUSTIN

President Scott B. Ransom joins Texas House Speaker Joe Straus and UNT Chancellor Lee Jackson as they review construction on the new Medical Education and Training Building in March 2009.

The lessons learned from the successful campaign to win state passage of Senate Bill 160, which added $150,000 to the bottom line, 40 years ago became internalized as standard operating procedure. These lessons can be summarized roughly as

- Do your homework; be able to point to similar pieces of legislation benefitting other institutions.
- Have a point person in the House and one in the Senate and help them line up the votes.
- Have your own point person and trusted figures on your side willing to write letters and make telephone calls.
- Make a persuasive case as to the benefits or even savings to the state.
- Put all funds received to good use and thereby be worthy in the future.

It's a formula that, with the addition of long years developing personal relationships, has worked time and time again for TCOM and the HSC, so well in fact that the HSC substantially leads the state's other health science centers in building space per student. It certainly helps when working with government to be able to partner with professional organizations such as the Texas Academy of Family Physicians, the Texas Association of Rural and Community Hospitals and the Texas Rural Health Association.

Danny Jensen has been the inheritor of this received wisdom for the past 25 fruitful years. The need for good relations with all levels of government is so great that Jensen serves as associate vice chancellor for Governmental Affairs for the UNT System. When he is not in his office in the EAD Building on the HSC campus in Fort Worth, he is usually at the UNT System office in Dallas or the one in Austin.

"When I look at buildings on campus, I see faces," says Jensen. "The Bio-Tech Building and the DNA Lab, I see Chris Harris in the Senate. Doubling the size of the campus and our newest building, I see Jane Nelson. In all of those cases, Charlie Geren carried the load in the House. The Patient Care Center was Mike Moncrief when he was a senator." The first building on campus, Medical Education Building 1, was built with federal funds helped along by Congressman Jim Wright in the mid-1970s. All subsequent campus improvements have depended on state appropriations.

Jensen emphasizes that, key as state appropriations are, the HSC works with all levels of government. "The other side of the coin," Jensen explains, "is helping elected officials do their job. If the mayor's office calls up wanting a speaker on Alzheimer's disease for the Women's Auxiliary meeting Wednesday night, we get them an expert speaker. If county health officers contact us needing physician screening for an emerging public health situation or a state representative gets called about who can provide last-minute physicals for a team here from out of state for a baseball tournament and in turn calls us, we make sure we come through for them."

Local US Reps. Michael Burgess, MD, and Kay Granger have worked closely with Jensen's office over recent years. "Granger and Burgess have been very active on our behalf," says Jensen. "Granger helped arrange the original funding from the FBI and our collaboration with them. With Burgess being a physician, he has instant credibility when he speaks for us. He has been particularly effective for us working with the National Institutes of Health."

Party label has not mattered at all over the years. Whether the Tarrant County state delegation has been all Democrat, all Republican or mixed, TCOM and the HSC have received the same strong support. Indeed, the fight for the most significant bill in TCOM history, Senate Bill 216, signed into law in May 1975, that associated TCOM with North Texas State University and brought a measure of state support, was led by the team of Democrat Gib Lewis in the House and Betty Andujar in the Senate, the first Republican elected from Tarrant County. The history of the HSC could have been quite different without the strong support received year-in and year-out from all levels of government. ◼

Centers of Excellence

The Health Institutes of Texas

"Bench to bedside." To researchers, that is the imperative to make new discoveries at the laboratory bench and move them with all prudent haste to the patient bedside. The units within the Health Science Center where the laboratory "rubber" really meets the bedside "road" are the Health Institutes of Texas (HIT), 12 innovation centers, some with multiple teams, charged with making serious dents in problems that hit Texas in the pocketbook and Texans in their quality of life. The findings that come from the Health Institutes of Texas, as you will see, don't just address needs of our state, but the world around.

HIT was designed to leverage our growing expertise in public health, interdisciplinary scientific research, medical education and health care delivery by

- Determining or refining the problem;
- Solving the problem using a multidisciplinary approach;
- Implementing the solutions through prevention and student and provider education; and
- Measuring outcomes.

The Health Institutes of Texas are "crucibles" where interdisciplinary teams can form, where theoretical and applied investigators work side-by-side, for the long or short term, to explore problems affecting people's health. But they are more than that. The institutes themselves are formed along different lines, some by type of disease or type of medical practice or type of technology. This fosters frequent collaboration between the institutes as well as within. On top of that, there is extensive need for communications and partnering with external entities — hospitals and research centers, practitioners and professional organizations, patients and patient groups, technology companies and medical suppliers, federal and local agencies.

The institutes had their beginning in 1992 with the founding of the North Texas Eye Research Institute by Thomas Yorio, PhD, in collaboration with Alcon, the leading producer of sterile ophthalmic products. The first five institutes — for vision, aging and Alzheimer's disease, cardiovascular disease, cancer and physical medicine — were known collectively in the nineties as The Institutes for Discovery. HIT was formalized in 2007. With numerous centers under its umbrella that encourage interdisciplinary collaboration.

The Texas Center for Health Disparities (TCHD) was formed in 2005 to address the fact that Texas's large minority populations suffer disproportionately from such scourges as diabetes, cardiovascular disease, stroke, infant mortality, cancer, tobacco-related diseases and HIV, with death rates from these causes rising to double and more that experienced in the non-Hispanic white

Cardiovascular Research Institute

Center for Commercialization of Fluorescence Technologies

Center for Community Health

Focused on Resources for her Health, Education and Research

Institute for Aging and Alzheimer's Disease Research

Institute for Cancer Research

Institute for Investigative Genetics

Mental Sciences Institute

North Texas Eye Research Institute

Osteopathic Research Center

Primary Care Research Institute

Texas Center for Health Disparities

HEALTH INSTITUTES OF TEXAS

Texas Center for Translational Research
Texas Center for Primary and Rural Care
Texas Center for Health Outcomes

▲

Abbott Clark directs the North Texas Eye Research Institute (NTERI).

population. The causes of this disparity are various — economics, lifestyle, genetics, location — and the need to investigate and redress these underlying issues is pressing.

Jamboor Vishwanatha, PhD, dean of the Graduate School of Biomedical Sciences, is director of the center. Robert Kaman, JD, PhD, associate dean of the GSBS, directs the Education and Training Core, which, through several programs, helps promising students and health professionals gain exposure to or participate in biomedical educational activities for underrepresented minorities.

School of Public Health alumna Kathryn Cardarelli, director of the Center for Community Health, works with minority communities to increase health awareness.

Outreach to communities, both to raise awareness of key health issues and to implement health improvement programs, is a vital role of TCHD. Kathryn Cardarelli, PhD, MPH, serves as director of the Outreach Core. She is also director of the Center for Community Health. Michael Smith, PhD, a professor of integrative physiology, directs the Research Core.

The **Cardiovascular Research Institute** (CRI) is one of many research centers in the world addressing the foremost health problem in North America (and the leading non-infectious medical issue worldwide). Roughly 60 million Americans, knowingly or not, are dealing with significant cardiovascular disease (CVD). In the United States, one-third of all men and one in 10 women die from heart attack or heart failure. This high morbidity combined with the types of surgical intervention common for dealing with advanced-stage CVD make it a disproportionately large chunk of our health care and health insurance costs. If that alone does not give CVD high research priority, there is also the fact that many strongly believe that its common forms will one day be largely eliminated by inexpensive preventive measures and treatments.

The CRI was formed in 1995, and Tom Cunningham, PhD, serves as its director today. Research takes place in five primary divisions and two adjunct divisions and covers prevention, diagnosis, treatment and rehabilitation of cardiovascular disease.

Partnering with and empowering communities provides the mission for the **Center for Community Health** (CCH), begun in 2007. Projects to date, primarily in Tarrant and Dallas counties, have addressed a wide array of issues, from information and awareness programs for birthing support in minority communities, to a prostitute diversion program seeking to break cycles of violence, substance abuse and sexually transmitted diseases, to cancer disparities and HPV vaccination drives, children's health and

wellness initiatives and a comprehensive mental health survey of North Texas.

The common threads uniting these diverse projects are to increase communities' awareness of and use of health resources available to them; to work in concert with key figures in communities to foster effective communication aimed at identifying and addressing health issues; and to empower communities to continue to take effective measures on their own behalf. Projects are analyzed in detail, from the raw health data to effectiveness of steps taken, in order to create paradigms of effective partnering and to identify issues with health-policy implications. Kathryn Cardarelli is the founding director of the center.

The field of photonics — the concept that we can harness photons just as we do electrons in electronics — started with the development of the laser in the 1960s. This led promptly to such medical innovations as laser surgery and endoscopy, but recent technical advances hold the promise of an abundance of life-saving and life-enhancing procedures. And why not — it promises noninvasive detection of minute changes down to the cellular or even molecular level. The mission of the **Center for Commercialization of Fluorescence Technologies** (CCFT) is to realize the potential of this protean technology by rapid prototyping of the necessary instruments, knowledge bases and applications.

The UNTHSC recruited internationally respected biophysicists Zygmunt "Karol" Gryczynski, PhD, brother Ignacy Gryczynski, PhD,

Tom Cunningham, right, directs the team of the Cardiovascular Research Institute.

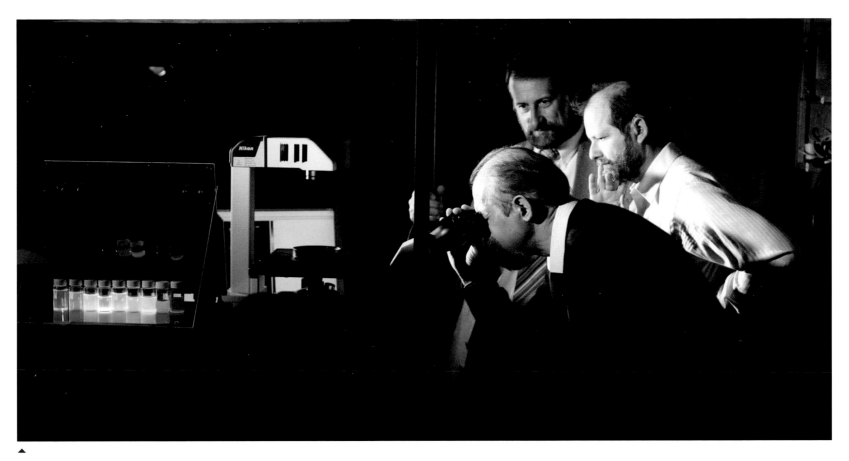

The Center for Commercialization of Fluorescence Technologies — Ignacy Gryczynski, brother Zygmunt Gryczynski and Julian Borejdo (l-r) — promises major life-saving discoveries.

Evgenia Matveeva, PhD, and Julian Borejdo, PhD, to found the center in 2006, funded by a legislative grant from the Emerging Technologies Fund (ETF) created by Gov. Rick Perry. Zygmunt Gryczynski is its current director.

Much of the center's research has been in the particular field of fluorescence spectroscopy, which uses a beam of light to stimulate the electrons in molecules to emit lower energy light, which is then measured and analyzed. The CCFT is at work on applications to detect biohazardous materials, to monitor glucose levels in diabetics and cardiac markers in heart patients as well as for early detection of prostate and breast cancers. The center also has as its mission serving as a resource to researchers in academia and industry worldwide in a variety of fluorescence-related technologies.

The FOR HER team of Peggy Smith-Barbaro, Meharvan "Sonny" Singh and Center Director Ralph Anderson concentrates on women's health.

Focused on Resources for her Health Education and Research (FOR HER), founded in 2007, attempts, through clinical services and research, to create a comprehensive model of women's health. Clinical Services, chaired by Ralph Anderson, MD, provides care to women in Tarrant County and beyond in the gamut of medical issues pertaining to women — breast and cervical cancer, menopause and hormones, pregnancy and birth, postpartum depression, infant mortality and obesity. Anderson also serves as FOR HER director.

FOR HER Research is chaired by Meharvan Singh, PhD, and focuses in the areas of postpartum/perinatal depression, biology of menopause, and hormone therapy and pregnancy outcomes including infant mortality. Peggy Smith-Barbaro, PhD, chairs the Education Committee, and the osteopathic students receive 200 hours in additional training on osteopathic manipulative medicine (OMM) that they then use in treating patients and supporting improved health. **The Osteopathic Research Center** (ORC) is tasked with providing an evidence base for osteopathic manipulation.

OMM represents a large body of manual therapy and even diagnostic techniques for the musculoskeletal system that date back to A. T. Still's discovery of osteopathic medicine in the 1870s. The efficacy of OMM won legions of devotees to osteopathic medicine in the early days, including in Fort Worth such storied residents as Amon G. Carter and Sid W. Richardson, which led in due course to much of the financial backing enjoyed by the Health Science Center.

With the boom in medical technology of the last century, manual therapy began to be seen as out-of-fashion if not, as a few argued, outright quackery. Even before that, the medical field began demanding evidence-based medicine; every procedure needed to prove its efficacy or be discarded. Osteopathic physicians, who time and again had witnessed patient benefits flow from OMM, were at the forefront of seeking evidential proof for its effectiveness. The national Osteopathic Research Center (ORC), on the campus of the Health Science Center, has led the way for the profession since 2001.

Now under the direction of John Licciardone, DO, MS, MBA, the ORC has conducted studies of specific manipulations, such as the lymphatic pump, used by osteopathic physicians at various points on the body to boost immune function and reduce edema, or swelling. A new AOA-funded study by Lisa Hodges, PhD, is exploring the

usefulness of this technique in treating breast cancer. That study is running concurrently with a larger NIH-funded study to evaluate the immune-function assist that lymphatic pump techniques provide. Other studies have explored OMM as a treatment on its own or as a complement to drug therapies for a wide variety of commonplace complaints — carpal tunnel syndrome, lower back pain, pregnancy, diabetes, ear infections, influenza and respiratory tract infections.

The ORC received a generous $1.1-million initial investment from the leading osteopathic professional organizations — the American Osteopathic Association, the American Association of Colleges of Osteopathic Medicine and the American Osteopathic Foundation. Substantial ongoing funding has been received from the Osteopathic Heritage Foundation and from the National Institutes of Health.

The most recent of the institutes, the **Institute for Investigative Genetics** (IIG) was formed in 2009 with the recruitment of Bruce Budowle, PhD, formerly senior scientist for the Federal Bureau of Investigation's forensics laboratory and a leading expert in bioterrorism and microbial forensics. The foremost project underway involves finding ways to obtain accurate assays when DNA evidence is too scant for existing techniques. Success will lead to a wide variety of applications, including, most prominently, forensics and missing persons identification. Another project involves the correlation of genetic markers to diseases and to physical traits. This could lead to opening up the promising field of genetic medicine

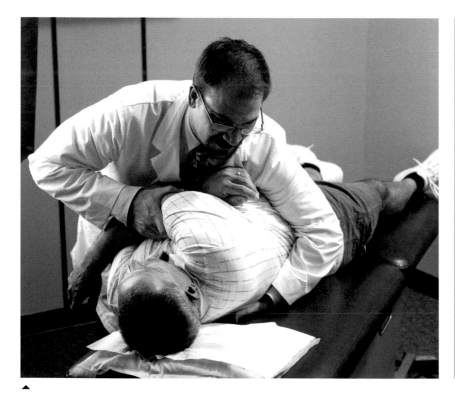

Assistant Professor Dennis E. Minotti of the Osteopathic Research Center on campus provides osteopathic manipulative therapy to a patient.

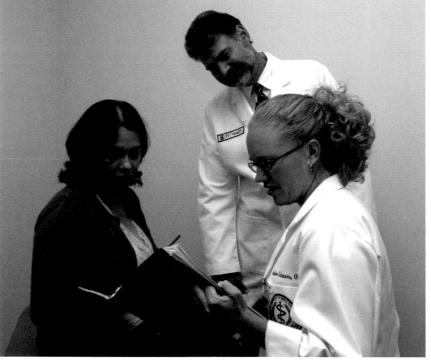

John Licciardone is director of the ORC and associate dean for clinical research.

Bruce Budowle (r) leads the Institute for Investigative Genetics teams.

and also to more precise autopsies and more precise appearance descriptions when the person who left the sample is unknown.

Three other research centers have been brought under the IIG. The Center for Human Identification has almost a decade of experience working with the FBI and other agencies and governments around the world to identify human remains. The Center for Biological Safety and Security employs the Health Science Center's mass spectrometry capability to improve methods of detecting and defending against biological weapons, such as ricin and anthrax, and other bio-terrorism threats and emerging diseases. The Center for Computational Genomics, under the direction of Ranajit Chakraborty, PhD, was founded in 2009 for advanced biostatistical and bioinformatic studies of genomes. Much of this research will be conducted in the area of inter-individual genetic variation, furthering the development of individualized medicine through better understanding how variation in disease susceptibility, drug response and reaction to environmental insult are linked to specific identifiable genetic markers.

Though perhaps the most publicized of the centers at UNTHSC, the UNT **Center for Human Identification** (CHI) has not traditionally been considered one of the Health Institutes of Texas. This is because its work is in the field of applied genetics — casework — rather than genetics research. However, CHI, directed by Art Eisenberg, PhD, recently was folded in under the new Institute for Investigative Genetics, outlined above, and the Texas Senate has requested that it be the home for tick-borne-disease testing and research. Furthermore, the entire field of forensic genetics has experienced growth demands way beyond what was foreseeable, and so out of necessity has demanded techniques for doing more faster with less.

This innovation effort has been organized into the Research and Development Laboratory, which has the goal of being able to analyze ever smaller and more degraded remains samples and, through

An Instance of Student-Initiated Research

Students are not blank slates. They bring their own backgrounds and issues, and from time to time these can become fodder for research. Here is a revealing case.

The UNT campus in Denton is home to a world-renowned music department. In 2008, Eri Yoshimura was a doctoral student there in piano performance. Her long hours at the keyboard were causing pain in her hands.

She approached Kris Chesky, PhD, head of UNT Denton's Texas Center for Music and Medicine, which is devoted primarily to preventing hearing loss in musicians. Yoshimura presented a survey she conducted a couple of years earlier that discovered it was rare for collegiate piano students to play without pain — 86 percent experienced pain to a degree that limited their amount of practice. One hunch that surfaced was that the problem lay in the fact that piano keyboards had long-since been designed for the hands of male performers, whereas the largest cohort of student pianists nowadays is Asian females.

Eri Yoshimura, piano performance doctoral student at the UNT Denton campus, studies data about hand positioning on piano keyboards.

Chesky then approached Rita Patterson, PhD, director of the Osteopathic Heritage Foundation Physical Medicine Core Research Facility (OHFPMCRF) at UNTHSC, to see if she would be interested in a study of the hand kinematics of piano players in the hope of finding a solution to the pain problem. She and Shrawan Kumar, PhD, an OHFPMCRF professor, were ready to help in Fort Worth, coincidentally hometown of the world-famous Van Cliburn International Piano Competition.

The result is a study of 30 student-pianists performing on a specially modified keyboard that can record the force with which keys are depressed. Together with measures of hand size and playing position and correlated with reports of discomfort — while playing and afterward — the study is yielding valuable insights for piano instruction as well as keyboard design.

Students from the Health Science Center's four schools now function in an atmosphere of multi-disciplinary collaboration employing the latest technologies, learning tools and team approaches, the better to equip them for success in today's dynamic health environment.

TOMORROW

Part of the contemporary medical paradigm is the belief that our toughest health problems will yield only to inter-professional approaches that unite the perspectives of relevant fields. The Health Science Center is consciously reshaping toward the goal of moving discoveries made at the laboratory bench rapidly to the patient bedside and on out to the community of health care providers and recipients, to the benefit of all.

UNT | HEALTH™
SCIENCE CENTER

Narrow focus has been a watchword in the development of capabilities as the UNTHSC seeks to develop specific areas of excellence, such as Cardiovascular Research, Aging and Alzheimer's, Investigative Genetics and Primary Care, each drawing on a wealth of talent to pursue its mission. Pictured is Tom Cunningham, director of the Cardiovascular Research Institute.

Research Awards – 2000-2015

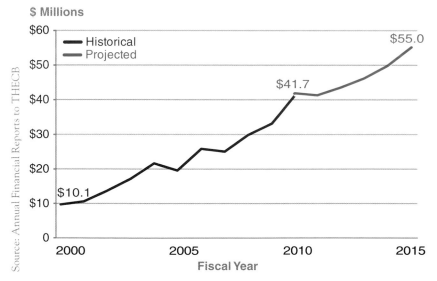

$ Millions

Source: Annual Financial Reports to THECB

— Historical
— Projected

$60

$55.0

$50

$41.7

$40

$30

$20

$10.1

$10

0

2000   2005   2010   2015

Fiscal Year

providers, and our graduates often receive offers of permanent jobs even before graduation. The plan for PA Studies is to grow from 170 students in 2010 to 235 students by 2016, a 38-percent increase.

Students in the Physical Therapy program, started in 2010, will prepare for a doctoral degree with a unique curriculum enhanced through academic partnership with osteopathic manipulative medicine, rural physician training and collaborative physical

medicine research. Physical Therapy is expected to grow from 30 students to 180 students by 2016, an impressive six-fold increase.

The largest and oldest of the schools to join TCOM on campus, our Graduate School of Biomedical Sciences, is led by Dean J. K. Vishwanatha. Much of the expected GSBS growth will come from the popular medical sciences degree program, designed to provide a track for students with a more diverse array of educational backgrounds to be able to enter and succeed in medical and other professional schools. We expect to grow from 175 students in 2010 to 190 by 2016 in that program alone, while total GSBS enrollment will expand from 355 students in 2010 to 425 by 2016, a 20-percent increase.

Naturally, the number of faculty in all our schools will need to grow concurrently so that we can maintain our excellent faculty/student ratio. Our plan will take us from 400 faculty members in 2010 to 472 by 2016, or an 18-percent growth.

Growing Research

Research will remain integral to reaching Top 10 status as well as provide a key source of institutional revenue going forward as state support is expected to shrink. We will continue to partner in new ways to speed lab discoveries to patient care delivery and transfer our discoveries to the marketplace.

Our research strategic growth plan, under the direction of Vice

Regents unanimously approve MD school proposal

MD Study Group Chair and former Fort Worth Mayor Kenneth Barr presents information to the UNT System Board of Regents in front of a packed Luibel Hall audience in March 2009.

On August 19, 2010, the UNT System Board of Regents unanimously voted to approve the development of a new MD degree program as an independent fifth school in addition to the Texas College of Osteopathic Medicine, Graduate School of Biomedical Sciences, School of Public Health and School of Health Professions.

Approval came on completion of pre-approval requirements the regents had directed UNTHSC leadership to accomplish at their November 2009 meeting. The requirements were to secure all necessary start-up funding from the community, establish a business plan for the new school, create commitments to secure a strong future for all existing programs and confirm relationships with area hospitals for student rotations and graduate training.

Over two years, UNTHSC conducted extensive fiscal and academic planning to determine how its existing infrastructure will optimally support two separately accredited medical programs and support interdisciplinary collaboration among campus programs. Thanks to this unique sharing opportunity, the business and academic plan estimated the start-up costs for the new MD program would total $21.5 million, substantially less than what would normally be estimated without existing infrastructure.

"This innovative private-public proposal is particularly important as the state responds to financial challenges by allowing the local community to provide all start-up funds for a new medical school as a method to address the growing physician shortages across the state," said President Scott Ransom.

The Fort Worth health care, business and civic community pledged more than $25 million to cover the initial incremental and all start-up costs. Written partnership agreements with nine hospitals as well as substantial financial pledges were obtained with Texas Health Resources, Tarrant County Hospital District, Baylor Health System, HCA North Texas/Plaza Medical Center and Cook Children's Health System.

"There is a great deal of excitement about this opportunity in Fort Worth as a logical progression of the Health Science Center's ongoing growth and success," said UNTHSC Foundation Board member George Pepper. "The Fort Worth community has demonstrated tremendous commitment, which now allows us to take this proposal forward."

At this printing, UNTHSC was preparing to finalize the accreditaion and approval process necessary to begin the new MD program.

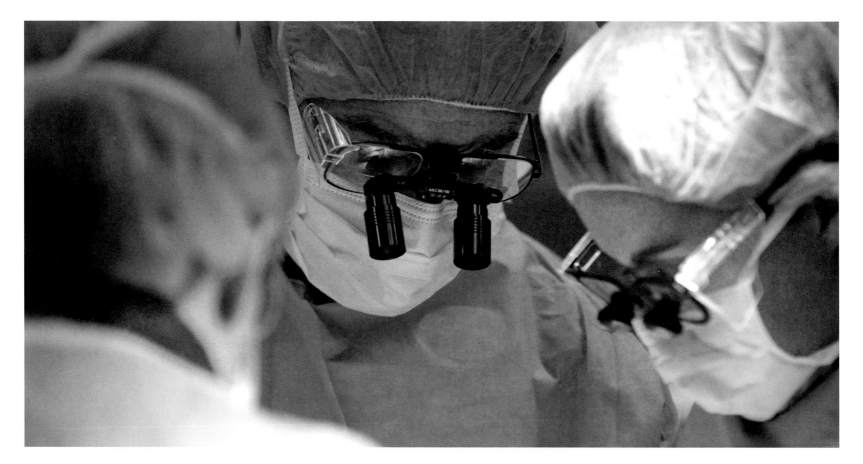

President Glenn Dillon, PhD, includes goals to recruit, develop and retain high-performing faculty; enhance facilities and infrastructure; invest in translational research capacity; and enhance and develop partnerships.

Extramural research expenditures are predicted to climb from a record $41.7 million in 2010 to more than $50 million in awards by 2016.

Growing Care Delivery

Much of the future revolution in medical care delivery will continue to focus on ways to get the right amount of the right care to the right people, swiftly yet affordably. The goals of UNT Health, our clinical-faculty practice under the direction of Executive Vice President of Clinical Affairs and Business Development for UNTHSC and President of UNT Health Kathleen Forbes, MD, are to continuously improve quality, access, service and patient satisfaction; optimize market and partnership opportunities; and take advantage of Affordable Care Act provisions.

Future plans include setting up a network of state-of-the-art multi-specialty care centers across Tarrant County and exploring additional new location options as well. The greater number of these centers, plus their expanded hours, will help satisfy the demand among residents of the county for more convenience and greater access to services.

Patient Encounters – 2000-2015

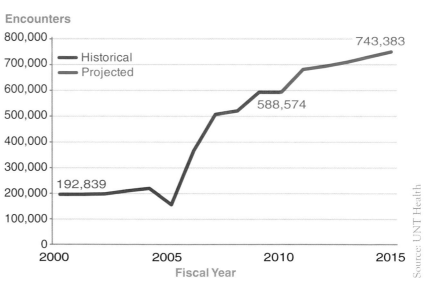

Source: UNT Health

Since 2000, UNT Health has grown to a thriving clinical enterprise that now provides 40 percent of institutional revenues. We plan to grow from almost 600,000 patient visits and $85 million in revenue in 2010 to approximately 743,000 patient visits and $100 million in revenue by 2016.

Solidifying our Focus

We do many wonderful things at the Health Science Center, but we know that a more streamlined focus will be key to our future success. In our strategic plan going forward, we will focus on those things we are absolutely best at — the "hard differentiators" that make us stand out in education, research and care — primary care and prevention; aging and Alzheimer's disease; and investigative genetics. Investment in these areas will help solidify our institution's position in the market.

The other two areas that will make our future success a reality are foundational to all parts of the organization — Administration and Community Engagement.

Growing our Administrative Capabilities

Naturally, such an expected influx of students and faculty will demand having more support staff. To reach Top 10 status among the nation's health science centers means we will need to retain and develop high-performing talent while attracting newcomers who are real difference-makers. Our people will need appropriate infrastructure.

Our strategic plan for administration requires that we support and enhance a culture of excellence, performance improvement and

Fulltime Faculty – 2000-2015

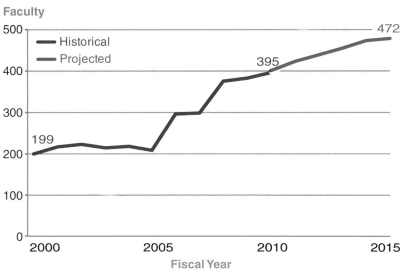

Source: Human Resources

accountability; ensure our facilities support our mission and promote a positive image; optimize financial resources; optimize information resources and infrastructure; promote faculty and staff diversity; and enhance human capital management.

Naturally, having more people demands having more floor space. Our strategic plan includes a Master Plan for the campus that will

add more square footage of that precious commodity and do so in a way that takes our reputation for innovation to a bold new level.

Growing Community Engagement

Central to the osteopathic tradition, and to the "Fort Worth Way," is the principle of partnership and collaboration — the world doesn't come to you; you have to go out into the world to make a difference. The ivory-tower mentality has never been our perspective, and we know it cannot exist in the future. Partnerships of all types are absolutely critical.

Community outreach and engagement has been an area of strength for the Health Science Center. It is a foundation on which we must be sure to build going forward. Our plan calls for us to continue to grow and build our reputation as a world-class institution; rapidly expand and strengthen our strategic alliances and partnerships; and diversify and strengthen our philanthropic and other revenue channels.

Even in the face of tough economic times in 2010, we have established a more ambitious future course than ever before. While it's aggressive, we know if we continue our tradition of hard work with a pioneering — if not a maverick — spirit, we will get the job done. For 40 years to date and for the future, one thing will never change — our long-standing commitment to the people of Texas and beyond.

Ruth Washington (center), senior administrative assistant in Human Resource Services, presents a donation from the Health Science Center's Campus Pride fund to the SafeHaven domestic violence program in honor of the late Makasha Colonvega, a TCOM student who died in 2009. Also pictured are Danna Wall, managing supervisor for the Berry Good Buys store, which benefits SafeHaven, and Susan Smith, assistant director of annual giving for the Health Science Center.

ROOM TO GROW

The New Campus Master Plan

By Greg Upp

The 27th of February, 2008, dawned and ended as a bittersweet day. It was the day designated to say a formal farewell to the building that had been home for almost 50 years to the Fort Worth Osteopathic Hospital (later the Osteopathic Medical Center of Texas, OMCT), the very building where the first Texas College of Osteopathic Medicine classes had met. The OMCT had factored heavily in selecting Fort Worth as the location for TCOM. When it shut down operations in 2004, a victim of changing economics, it is no exaggeration to say the OMCT had been a mainstay of two generations of newly minted osteopathic physicians as well as pretty much all of the osteopathic practitioners in the Fort Worth region.

When the OMCT closed its doors in 2004, the UNTHSC soon bought the 15-acre parcel adjacent to our campus, increasing total campus size by almost double and providing much-needed room for expansion. Planning for just how to expand had commenced almost immediately, beginning with the certainty that removal of the old hospital would proceed in an environmentally-aware manner that would see it become "organ donor" to construction projects around the region with very little needing burial in a landfill. Already, as we stood there on a bright, warm winter day, the non-structural interior of the building had been entirely salvaged and carted away. In less than six months, every vestige of the OMCT would be gone, and earth-moving equipment would arrive to begin the excavation for the Medical Education and Training Building, the first step in implementing our new 15-year Master Plan.

Planning begets planning

The Health Science Center's strategic plan recognizes that student and faculty numbers in our academic programs will grow by two-thirds in the near future. The specifics of addressing the physical demands of such expansion becomes the province of the campus Master Plan, and the requirements go well beyond the mere increase in raw numbers. We looked to enhance the physical beauty of the campus so that people would enjoy studying and working here. We needed to provide for the many advances in medical, research and educational technologies. As a multi-disciplinary institution, we wanted to physically provide for more cross-fertilization of minds. We also were keen to reflect our location facing Fort Worth's lovely Cultural District. The list goes on: traffic and parking, easements, campus topography, "wayfinding," vistas, storm planning, funding vagaries and more.

We selected Carter::Burgess (since acquired by Jacobs) and Polshek Partnership Architects to assist us in the planning, and we

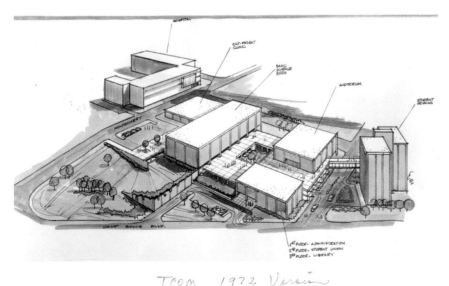

The Master Plan concept from 1972 projected a future Cultural District campus for TCOM.

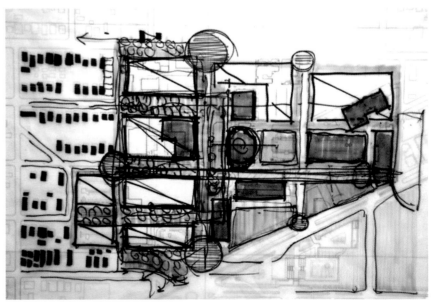

An early sketch from today's planning highlights a "campus spine" and "view corridors."

Ed Bass, gesturing, was among community members providing input to the Master Plan.

began by opening the process with input from neighbors and other interested parties. The plan that evolved would deliver more than 1 million square feet of new classroom and office space in accordance with the many other considerations that surfaced. Quickly, the planning sorted itself out into distinct phases.

Phase I

Phase I of the plan, scheduled to be completed by 2013 includes:

- Construction of two new buildings to be built on the site of the old OMCT. The Medical Education and Training Building, at 112,000 square feet and five floors, was opened in fall of 2010. Building B, planned for up to 100,000 square feet, awaits a funding go-ahead.
- Renovation of the OMCT parking structure allowed a reopening in May 2010.
- Changes to Montgomery Street. Formerly marking the western edge of campus, it will remain a public throughway but become tree-lined and pedestrian-friendly. As it now becomes a new major entrance to the campus from Camp Bowie Boulevard, signage, landscaping and entry treatments will be added.
- Removal of two one-story buildings between Montgomery and the Lewis Library with a courtyard and water feature added to enhance the campus community.
- Greening. To provide more of a collegiate feel, a quad will be constructed on the north side of the Medical Education and Training Building.

The Medical Education and Training Building had two different webcams focused on it during its construction so that all could track progress. Two 250-seat auditoriums that can be combined into one occupy the ground floor along with size-flexible conference areas and a café-style dining area. A 35-foot atrium separates the two-story auditoriums from a smaller second floor containing additional meeting and classroom space. The third floor is home to the much-needed administrative offices. The fourth floor houses both an osteopathic manipulative medicine training facility and a patient-simulator training room, and the fifth floor is the domain of the new Physical Therapy program. All of these rooms feature state-of-the-art electronics and the latest in educational technology.

Building B will be devoted to wellness and health, with recreation and fitness facilities, a faculty lounge and healthy food services. It will be sited along Haskell Avenue just to the west of the Medical Education and Training Building.

Future Phases

The final stages of the plan will carry us into the future. The main features that will be added to the Health Science Center campus include:

- Ten additional new buildings, beginning with Building H, a 150,000-square-foot research facility to be located on the campus' east end.
- A total of four campus quads.
- Six on-campus garden areas.
- New signage and wayfinding features throughout the campus.
- Landscaping suiting the Health Science Center's location in the Cultural District, including themed gardens, to be built at locations around the campus. These will serve as relaxation spots for HSC staff, faculty, students and visitors.
- Unobtrusive parking to accommodate the growing population.
- A central "spine" walkway designed to unify the west and east ends of campus.

Naturally, all of this construction demands that our utility infrastructure keep pace through both phases so that everything from air conditioning to power to drinking water to illumination is available as needed. Together, all the elements of the plan will accommodate our expected rapid growth of people and programs and will help fulfill our strategic goal of becoming a Top 10 health science center. ▨

From obtaining input from many audiences to the demolition of the OMCT to opening day of classes, the Medical Education and Training Building was a group effort.

Right page, clockwise: Medical students weigh in on designs. Carl Everett receives well wishes at the farewell. The new building's skeleton rises. The OMCT comes down. DOs Mel Johnson and Nelda Cunniff say their goodbyes.

Above left: Finishing touches to the MET exterior commence.

Right: Students help with greening around the new building. Here, students break in one of the two new 250-seat high-tech lecture halls in summer 2010.

The new MET building, left and above, is the first step in the institution's 15-year Master Plan.

Below: The MET is "Building A" on the Master Plan overview drawing. Current buildings are in dark gray.

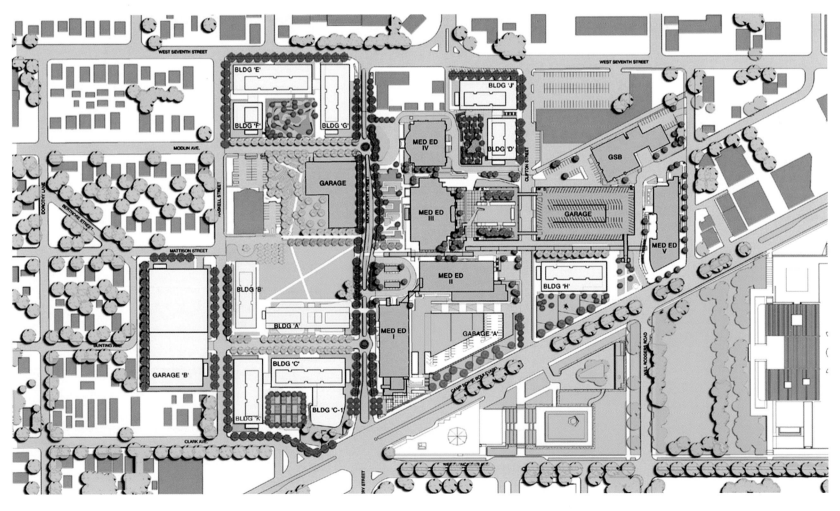

Environmentally Sensitive Growth

Throughout the development of the HSC Master Plan, we have been acutely sensitive to environmental considerations, from the "greening" of the campus to landscaping to help us blend and reflect well on our surroundings to traffic "calming." But perhaps no undertaking points to our commitment more than the demolition of the old Osteopathic Medical Center of Texas building and construction of The Medical Education and Training Building.

We turned to the US Green Building Council for LEED, or Leadership in Energy and Environmental Design, certification. Among the many standards we thereby elected to employ was a requirement that at least 75 percent of materials by weight be recycled. We bested that by recycling more than 2,000 truckloads of reusable materials:

- 2,637 tons of steel, aluminum and copper
- 6,435 tons of concrete
- 17,228 tons of masonry

In addition, we donated four crates of medical supplies to the River Oaks Volunteer Fire Department and all types of furniture, office equipment and fixtures, even medical and office supplies, to various local churches, school districts, universities and social service agencies.

The Medical Education and Training Building's design incorporated the mature trees protected during the demolition. The additional requirements of LEED certification assure that the building provides an environmentally responsible and healthy place to work.

Adapting While Leading

Pioneering the future of health care – a postscript

By Thomas Yorio, PhD

It was a blistering hot day in the summer of 1977 when my young family and I pulled into Denton, Texas, to begin our long association with Texas College of Osteopathic Medicine and, subsequently, the University of North Texas Health Science Center. Having come from New York City and Mount Sinai School of Medicine, we knew we were in for a change, not only because of the weather, but also because of the opportunity before us in joining this rather new, small, state-supported osteopathic medical school.

What I did not expect was just how quickly we were going to have to adjust and adapt. Texas was growing, and our institution was growing in tandem. Dr Ralph Willard, who was dean at the time and later became the second president, communicated a clear vision for TCOM to become the preeminent osteopathic college in the nation. He was leading the process of completing Medical Education Building 1 to house the burgeoning medical school. Within the year, we moved from limited space on the Denton UNT campus to interim space in the River Plaza office park by the Trinity River in Fort Worth close to where we could watch our new facility rise from the ground. In October of 1978, we moved into "Med Ed 1," the brand-new facility on the hill opposite the osteopathic hospital and across from the Amon Carter Museum. One year, two moves, before my research lab settled into a permanent home in what is now called the EAD.

Even as far back as the late 1970s, we knew we had to have a robust research program, not only to compete with our peer institutions in Texas for precious funds but to be able to approach research problems with diverse talent. Gordon Skinner, associate dean for Basic Sciences, emphasized how imperative it was to recruit individuals who were active researchers, not just academics. President Willard too had made clear his vision of the need to progress to becoming more a part of a university, as the osteopathic school where he had taught, Michigan State, had been.

Within the first year of my arrival, grant applications multiplied, and many of us were fortunate to obtain NIH and other grant support that afforded us increasing capability in basic science research and, in turn, enabled us to attract yet other leading researchers. Some of us were asked to get involved in the planning of the new facility's laboratories, which led to a number of labs being designed to accommodate the individual preferences of many of the researchers.

Getting involved early in the development of TCOM and its expansion into a full-fledged health science center was truly exciting for me as a new faculty member. With our new facility situated across the street from the Fort Worth Osteopathic Hospital, fondly known as the "O," we were able to attract an aspiring group of clinical faculty and to jump-start our practice plan. The growth in clinical faculty was needed to support the clinical training for our students. These were heady times, a feeling of ferment and excitement at having the opportunity to attract more colleagues and to expand the clinical and research programs in directions we felt they must go.

Texas had proved to me it was a state that would put ample resources behind its desire to improve health education and clinical care as we steadily received the funding to enhance our educational and research missions. But state funding was not a given; it tended to flow towards those institutions producing the best results. That had the effect of focusing us on producing excellence, a challenge as osteopathic medicine tended to be poorly understood or even misunderstood in Texas, as elsewhere. We struggled in our early efforts to get into universities for recruitment of students but soon began to attract more academically strong candidates. Our ability to garner research grants and our plans for campus growth also helped earn us state funding. In 1982, the basic science research building, Med Ed 2, was completed, which finally provided the requisite facilities for what I saw to be the critical step in the evolution of TCOM — from a state-supported osteopathic medical school into an academic health science center with a strong emphasis on research. The institution's recognition of the essential role for basic and clinical research in educating well-trained primary care physicians was first publicly expressed in 1984 in its research goals statement.

When Dr David Richards assumed the position of President of TCOM, we were already on our way to becoming the osteopathic medical school that others wanted to emulate. Not only were our students earning recognition for their high board scores and performances post-degree, but our faculty was making contributions in research that brought national and international attention.

This foundation allowed us to progress to the point where in 1993 Dr Richards went to the Texas Legislature to request for us to

UNT | HEALTH SCIENCE CENTER™

All UNTHSC schools contribute to research. Shown here, Eric Johnson of the School of Public Health.

positive changes." Dr George Luibel added, "The University of North Texas is a major university, and the designation will help TCOM receive additional recognition throughout the country. Despite these changes, our medical school is not going away. We will still be the singular source for an osteopathic medical degree in Texas." Their words still ring true today as we see that TCOM has not only benefited from this change but has grown into the leading osteopathic school in the nation.

In 1995, the local Fort Worth community approached us to consider adding a school of public health to the Health Science Center. A committee led by Leon Brachman served as one of the first focused community advisory bodies to the young Health Science Center. I was asked as Dean of the Graduate School to help bring in the first program for this potential school, the Master of Public Health (MPH). That degree program was approved in 1995 and was operational within the Graduate School of Biomedical Sciences. In 1999, we gained support from the Texas Higher Education Coordinating Board to start our new School of Public Health, and the MPH degree was moved into this new school. The addition of the School of Public Health has put us in the position of being one of two centers in Texas with medical, basic science and public health faculty and students sharing the same campus.

Bringing these different health-professions schools together has permitted us to create truly multidisciplinary and interdisciplinary institutes that focus on specific issues and areas of health needs. The creation of the Health Science Center was an innovation designed to meet the health needs of the growing population in Texas, the United States and the world. While it has taken a while in many cases for team members from differing disciplines to find a common language with which to discuss an issue, the payoff now is being able to approach the great health challenges of our time with the gamut of professional perspectives contributing to their solution.

In becoming a health science center, we have added a Graduate School of Biomedical Sciences, a School of Public Health and a School of Health Professions. These additions have enriched the educational environment; they have allowed many of our students to earn dual degrees; they have provided the community with choices in pursuing health careers; and they have enhanced our clinical

become one of the state's health science centers by the addition of the Graduate School of Biomedical Sciences (GSBS). That idea had been brewing for years, but the new administration undertook the heavy lifting of creating the detailed plan and winning approval and funding for it. The administration also had a vision to add other schools to the Health Science Center to further enrich the environment and to expand the mix of health professionals we were graduating. We wanted educational opportunities not only for osteopathic medical students on campus but also for those in the community who want to be able to stay close to home while pursuing other health-related degrees. This would, in turn, expose our medical students to a wider range of health perspectives.

The expansion into a health science center generated concerns from the local osteopathic community, which asked, "What will happen to TCOM?" and "Will TCOM retain its osteopathic identity?" However, the revered founding fathers of TCOM did not share the concern. Like the visionaries they were, they saw the change as a positive for TCOM. Dr Carl Everett said, "I would never have dreamed that we would make this much progress in a little more than 20 years. This is such a major step in TCOM's development that right now it's hard to comprehend all the advantages. The osteopathic profession will certainly benefit from the added recognition. It makes me feel good to see us making

Research engineer Sam Durham demonstrates sensors used to record and measure hand movements and musculoskeletal function.

As one aspect of this, recently the UNT System Regents unanimously approved finalizing the necessary steps to add an MD school as part of the Health Science Center. Why, when we already have a DO medical school? Texas remains among the most medically underserved areas in the nation. The decision has been received with some evident concern from a few in the Texas osteopathic community, similar to the concern expressed when the GSBS was added. But we have listened to our hospital partners who have expressed their desire to develop more ACGME (that is, MD) residencies and to form an agreement with an LCME (also MD) accredited institution for student clerkship learning opportunities. We decided that TCOM and the entire HSC would greatly benefit in becoming that partner and thus continue to have opportunities for all our students to remain locally for their clerkship training and potential residency programs. We believe establishing an MD school will enhance our educational environment, provide opportunities for students in our community and help support the infrastructure costs for our entire institution, while multiplying and augmenting training opportunities locally for our DO, MD, PA and PT students.

Bold? Yes. Controversial? Yes. But bringing an MD school under the HSC umbrella is, in the final analysis, an optimal pathway to a strong future. This will support the needs of our students, our local community, our parent institution and the state's population and even, I would argue, osteopathic medicine itself, making certain it remains front-and-center in any discussion of the future of health. In that case, what are the more general problems and opportunities we expect to hand off to the coming generation of clinicians, researchers and health administrators?

Health care reforms at the national and state levels will challenge our patient care system and indeed put more pressures on care providers, hospitals and health centers.

effectiveness. Our Health Institutes of Texas, multidisciplinary and interdisciplinary research centers of excellence, have provided a forum for the interchange of ideas, for innovation in research and for translation of these findings into treatment for our patients.

Today, we stand as the preeminent osteopathic medical school in the nation, and, yet, we are so much more. Not only do we have four excellent professional schools, we also have developed outstanding national and international reputations in the research of aging and Alzheimer's disease, cardiovascular disease, vision and osteopathic manipulative medicine, to name a few. Many of our schools' departments and programs have risen in recent years to be among the most respected in the country. Such recognition has not been obtained easily but has resulted from the dedication and hard work of students, faculty, staff and volunteers. We are proud of our accomplishments and recognize that our ability to adapt to the changing environment has led to much of our success.

From a small independent private medical college to becoming a health science center that is part of a university system, the University of North Texas System, with national recognition within just 40 short years is a remarkable story. However, our journey is only beginning. We know that we have obligations to our community to provide the highest standard of education and to create and deliver the most effective health care possible. We must look ahead to what the future will bring and then adapt and position ourselves to meet these needs.

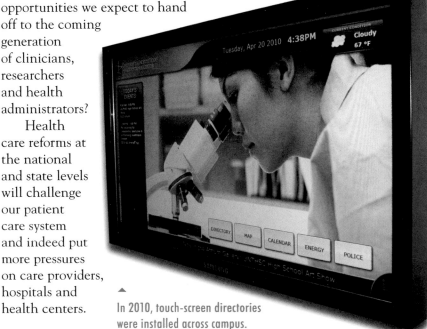

In 2010, touch-screen directories were installed across campus.

We need to do much more to position ourselves to be a positive influence on how this will happen and to make positive contributions to shape the economics and effectiveness of health care delivery in the future.

We must innovate new methods for educating physicians, physician extenders, therapists, scientists and community health workers to meet these needs. We need to take advantage of promising new technology in the delivery of our educational programs by incorporating avatars, holograms, 3-D video imaging and high tech computing to provide leadership in developing tomorrow's educational curriculum. We also need to have a seamless electronic patient record system so we can become true partners with our neighboring hospitals, allowing our patients to move within the health care system with ease while at the same time making it easy to bring the necessary expertise to bear on tough cases, even if that expertise is halfway around the world.

As a nation, we need to move from a health care system that focuses on treating acute and chronic illness to one that rewards an emphasis on health promotion and disease prevention. To do so will require major changes in how we educate our students, kindergarten through college, and train our health care providers, as well as bringing about major changes in our lifestyles. Such results will not be easily realized, but then again, we have not gotten to this point in our history taking the easy road.

Already, however, our faculty and students are clear, up-to-date and engaged on the issues we will face in the near future. In the final analysis, what is it that we health science administrators can do to make the future brighter for all? Yes, we can continue seeking out the best students, and we can perhaps even devise new curriculum and new learning methods. We can see to it that additional task-relevant knowledge can be instantly obtained, a button click away. We can ensure students learn in an environment peopled by a variety of disciplines, approaching problems from varied points of view. We can perhaps even make them more flexibly minded, more open to new methods and innovation.

However, none of this will work unless we allow future clinicians, researchers, faculty and administrators the opportunity to shape the future with the same zeal and fervor that I and my colleagues felt when we got our starts at TCOM in the late 1970s. It most certainly is our vital mission to provide an environment that inspires all of us to bring all our energy and brilliance to bear, tackling the key issues of science and medicine and charting the future growth and missions of this great institution.

We have come a long way from the first day of class in 1970 and have adapted to the changing environment with positive outcomes. We continue to provide an outstanding education to all our students. While we celebrate 40 years of success for TCOM and the Health Science Center, we must not forget that what inspired us was the chance to make a real difference, to do work that mattered in the great scheme of things. That is the one ingredient we cannot fail to provide. We must realize that after 40 years, we are still beginning.

I would love to be around to see what we will accomplish in the next 40 years. ▨

The new Physical Therapy program opened in 2010 with 30 students. Above, Michael Connors will teach using the latest equipment, such as an anti-gravity treadmill.